Big Time Opportunities and Strategies That Turn Pennies into Millions

Big Time Opportunities and Strategies That Turn Pennies into Millions

FORREST H. FRANTZ, SR.

Parker Publishing Company, Inc.
West Nyack, New York

© 1973 *by*

PARKER PUBLISHING COMPANY, INC.

West Nyack, N. Y.

Library of Congress Cataloging in Publication Data

Frantz, Forrest H
   Big time opportunities and strategies that turn
pennies into millions.

   1. Success. 2. Business. I. Title.
HF5386.F759   658.4'09   72-12931
ISBN 0-13-076307-1

INTRODUCTION

STRIKE IT RICH IN YOUR OWN BUSINESS

220,000 successful businesses are started each year. Someone just started a business (that may make him a millionaire) while you were reading this!

You can strike it rich in your own business. You don't need a lot of cash. Pennies will get you started. You can be worth hundreds of thousands — even become a millionaire — in less than five years. Increase your income, raise your standard of living and your prestige in your community in a matter of months. Never worry about your salary, pay cuts or layoffs again. Join the men who stand at the center of the American system and have true power and control — the businessmen of America. Taste the respect and prestige that people hold for men who control their own destinies and start their own enterprises. You'll experience all of this in your own business.

You can succeed in business regardless of your background, age, or physical condition. An average mind is all you need to forge ahead with this book into a successful business career.

If 220,000 people can start a successful business every year, so can you. Good luck. But if you master the principles in this book, you won't need it.

HOW TO BUILD A FORTUNE IN BUSINESS

Use this book as your guide and counselor. You'll take a fast tour of discovery in a new, practical, exciting world of prosperous investment and business during your first fast reading. Then, as you settle down to serious study, this book will help you select from several businesses well suited to you and your means. You'll learn how to get your business started with step-by-step instructions. You'll discover how to finance your business and how to promote and sell your way to riches quickly, easily, and automatically.

The first chapter gets right to the point with smart business strategies and introduces you to the ten big profit horizons containing every kind of business that has ever existed. Learn how a $50 investment built a million dollar business and how three other men started their own businesses on peanuts.

Chapter Two will really open your eyes by showing you how to turn a $20 bill into $100 to $500 worth of saleable product or a lifetime moneymaking career. I'll show you how to use almost anything you have laying around the house to start your own business and help you discover assets that you probably don't know you have. Ten examples show you how others started businesses of their own with $20 or less. This chapter (as well as those which follow) contains numerous business opportunity ideas and strategy checklists.

Perhaps you've got as much as $500 to start with. Then (or as soon as you've made your first $500) Chapter Three will guide you further. There's plenty of meat in this chapter on a host of businesses and techniques.

In Chapter Four you'll discover how to make money without

investing a penny. You'll learn about resources that I call "x," "y," and "z," with earning power of $5 to thousands of dollars (you read it right — thousands!) an hour, and how to cash in on them.

In Chapter Five you take the business selection test and evaluate yourself on the business selection matrix. You'll be counseled in business selection strategies that cull out the dull and poor ones before you start so you can avoid wasting years of frustration and possible eventual ruin.

In Chapter Six you'll discover how to raise large amounts of capital easily — how a mechanic of modest means did it. Where to borrow, what to use as collateral, how to sell a banker, other ways to raise capital, and how to prepare a financial statement are just a few of the subjects I'll cover in that chapter.

Many people are afraid to go into business because they don't know how to start. Chapter Seven tells you how to start in sixteen simple steps. We'll also explore the charactistics of people who succeed in business. This is a real "inside" look.

Chapter Eight will help you clinch your business success. You'll gain new insights on sales, promotion, advertising, and free publicity techniques that have made millions for big corporations and hundreds of thousands for small businesses.

Chapter Nine reveals the tactics that successful businessmen use to maximize profits. You'll learn how to buy at fantastically low prices, ways to trim expenses to the bone, and how to get highest prices. Did you know that you could have a prestige business address for only a few dollars a month? Study "front" tactics in Chapter Nine.

At this point you're ready for bigger things, and in Chapter Ten we get into big time wheeling and dealing. Chapter Eleven shows you how to cope with hard times, rough competition and adverse circumstances. Then, in Chapter Twelve, you get the graduate course in wheeling and dealing. The fabulous returns (half a million on a $50 investment) and the speedy cash pullouts ($10,000 cash in thirty days with no investment) are almost unbelievable. Yet they happen every day.

You'll learn about short-term launching pads, refinancing for cash pullouts, trading on the equity, "piece of the action" sweeteners, how to discover big deals, and how to assemble and promote big deals. Read carefully. Your opportunity to work one of these big deals may blossom tomorrow!

Forrest H. Frantz, Sr.

CONTENTS

11

CHAPTER 3 — Make Thousands Fast With

A $500 start gives you a big advantage • Send up a trial balloon • One-time profit ventures that you can start with $500 or less • Businesses that you can start with $500 or less • Hedge to minimize chance • Turn $500 into thousands in as little as one month • Small chips become multi-million dollar businesses • Tremendous profits in fifteen days • Your budget is a key factor • Make every cent count • Go where the action is • Don't piddle with two-bit ventures.

CHAPTER 4 — Make Hundreds Of Dollars

You don't need a cent to start • Use resource X to make $5 to $50 an hour • Resource Y can earn $5 to $200 an hour • Resource Z is worth $10 to $1000 an hour • X plus Z can earn $50 to $1,000,000 an hour • Opportunities that you can harness with resource X • Ways to capitalize on resource Y • How to cash in on resource Z • How to develop your resource Y • A daily plan for sharpening resource Z • Start a notebook • Make firm decisions.

CHAPTER 5 — A Foolproof Strategy For
Selecting Your Quick-Profit

Choose the right business and reap a bundle • The ten question business selection test • The Selection Matrix • How to get the deal that fits you best • Pick big-profit ventures • Find a repeater • Get a high percentage return on investment cash • Pick a business that attracts capital • Minimize your risk • Keep it easy to manage • How to get in for the lowest dollar • Security/profit trade-offs • Last, but foremost • Your three major objectives.

Dennis R.'s $100 next egg got him into a $10,000 business • How to get lots of money with a small nest egg • The basic methods for financing your successful business • Where to borrow money and get credit • The pros and cons of debt

How to Get Starting Capital Easily (cont.)

and equity financing • Make your banker want to lend you more money • Prepare a growth progress report • Compensating balances • Five techniques for building increasing credit • How to get paid for what you sell or lend • Syndicates, joint ventures and corporations simplified • How to form your own corporation • Where to look for equity investors.

Get off to a good start • Step 1: Develop the concept of your business and study the field • Step 2: Determine real estate, equipment, inventory, employee and other requirements • Step 3: Determine the start-up cost • Step 4: Make a market survey • Step 5: Determine your share of the market • Step 6: Prepare a cash flow projection • Step 7: Analyze the results of the first seven steps • Step 8: Seek disinterested counsel • Step 9: Obtain financing and determine equipment and inventory delivery possibilities • Step 10: Find a building or space for the business • Step 11: Place equipment and inventory orders • Step 12: Recruit employees • Step 13: Prepare opening promotion campaign • Step 14: Obtain licenses and permits required • Step 15: Equip and stock the business • Step 16: Open for business • What makes people succeed in business.

Blake L. tripled his income in three months • Good salesmanship spells profit in any business • Six ways to convert timid, uncolorful people into top salesmen • Develop selling points for your product • Six steps to making a sale • How to get attention and break preoccupation • The way to create desire to buy • How to make the prospect help to sell himself • How to pyramid the product value in the prospect's mind • Proof and confidence building that clinches sales • The step that poor salesmen forget • Handling objections • How to synthesize your business image • Promotion plans that build the image • Foolproof busi-

Techniques That Keep The Cash Rolling In (cont.)

ness opening promotion techniques • How to write ads that sell • How to get free publicity.

Profit is what you keep • Sell or trade for the highest price • Buy at rock bottom prices • Save $300 to $1000 a month on location • "Front" tactics that will put your home business uptown • Cut overhead with services that cost only when working • Money-saving equipment ideas • How to find a low-cost business location • Cost sharing • Rent, buy, or build? • Twenty-eight ways to cut expenses • How to reduce maintenance costs • How to profit on fifty years' experience in two hours • Where to get inexpensive publications on specific businesses • Small business administration services • What your accountant can do for you • What your banker can teach you • Other sources of business counsel and information.

Merlin K. becomes a wheeler-dealer • New big dollar profits are yours • Make sizeable profits in construction • The secrets of buy-rent • Tap real estate capital gains • Form and profit from syndicates • Earn big returns • Pick profitable equity investments • Lend money for profit • How to make good deals come your way • Use financial skill to increase margins • Sure deals in the stock market • How to gain expertise in the stock market • Keep emotion out of big deals • Keep your money turning • Eyeball the future • Get and use inside information.

Why opportunities are greater when times are bad • Ways to increase net worth in bad times • How to outsell competitors in bad times • Cut overhead in bad times • Turn adverse conditions in to opportunities • Counterattack

**Get Rich In Spite Of Adversity, Hard Times,
And Fierce Competition (cont.)**

strategy for adversity • How to overcome fierce competition
• What to do when your competitor undersells you • The
mind over matter concept • How I plunged ahead in spite
of staggering odds • The icebox treatment • When and how
to change course.

**CHAPTER 12 — The Mechanics Of

Wheeler-dealers make big profits • Know-how essential to
wheeler-dealing • Fifteen keys to wheeler-dealer success
• How Baxter R. financed his start • Short-term launching
pads • Refinance for tax-free cash pull-outs • Trade on the
equity • Wheeler-dealers program and manage debt • Debt
mechanics in sale-purchase • How to get interest below
prime • "Piece of the action" sweeteners • Wheeler-dealers
are promoters • How to discover potential big deals • How
to package and promote big deals • Keep yourself motivated with goals • Incentive programs start at home.

Chapter 1

TEN BIG PROFIT VENTURE
AREAS WITH 100,000
BUSINESS OPPORTUNITIES

YOU CAN STRIKE IT RICH!

There is a boundless horizon of opportunities waiting for men and women with courage and fortitude. You need not be rich to tap one or several of these opportunities; you need not have special talents or special connections to win great wealth. There is little or no risk involved, and in some instances the demands on your time are so small that you can successfully conduct several ventures simultaneously.

There are approximately 12 million recognized businesses in the United States. In addition to these, there are millions of home, part-time businesses and business-associated activities. The 12 million businesses recognized by the Treasury Department now have grown from only 6-1/2 million businesses twenty-five years ago. Thus, approximately 5-1/2 million businesses have been started during the last twenty-five years — most of them by someone like yourself.

There are only four things that you have to do in order to cross the bridge to wealth, riches, independence, and greater happiness in life.

First: Make up your mind to move ahead in your own business.

Second: Develop a plan that identifies the business that you're going to go into and the way you're going to conduct it.

Third: Go ahead and do it.

Fourth: Step to continuing income by operating your business at a profit in spite of odds and temporary setbacks.

It's all there waiting for you. You can strike it rich — but, you have to do it yourself. No one else will do it for you!

START WITH VERY LITTLE OR NO MONEY

It doesn't take a lot of money to start your own business venture. There are many businesses that you can enter without investing a single penny. There are others that you can get into with investments of only a few pennies or a few dollars. Even businesses that might seem to require thousands of dollars to start can be started with very small (or no) investment at all by the enterprising, big-time opportunity-oriented individual.

In this chapter you'll learn how Harry K. started his business with seventy-five cents. He now enjoys an income of $25,000 a year. Blaine U. started his electronics company with $75. He did $100,000 in business during his first year. Clara N., a friend of mine, started a novel sewing center with only a few hundred dollars. Within a year she was operating five sewing centers. Three enterprising young men in Dallas started a greeting card company with $200. In five years they were doing several million dollars' business annually. Mr. and Mrs. C. started a wedding consulting and catering service in their kitchen. Now they have a fashionable downtown store. Mort S. invested in a postage stamp to start a successful manufacturer's representative business.

Unusual? No. These are typical success sequences that are maturing around you every day. You don't have to start with much money. This minimizes your risk and possible loss, and it also tends to make a more resourceful and successful businessman out of you. Consequently, when you've grown your business into the big chips, you can wheel and deal in larger units of money more wisely and with surer chances of success.

How much do you have to start your business? Whether it's 10¢, $10, $100, $1000, or $10,000, there are opportunities galore. This book will help you to discover thousands of big time opportunities that will fit your business ambitions, no matter how meager or large. You'll discover strategies, techniques, and ideas that will help you turn pennies into nundreds, thousands, and more. If you have what it takes — and many people do — and if you'll work at it, you can join the millionaire's club in a few short years.

USE SMART BUSINESS STRATEGIES

Use smart business strategies and proven know-how to make your business venture a booming success. You'll learn these strategies and acquire the know-how from this book. The businesses that grow fast and make big money are run by people who acquire know-how, put it to work, and push through to success under any and all circumstances.

Take time now, before you invest a penny, to get this sure-profit know-how. Every minute you put into the study of business principles, techniques, and strategies now will make many dollars for you in the future. In this book, I've tried to provide a manual for building your own business empire quickly. I've tried to present a gold mine of business information that can be absorbed in a minimum of time. If you study, understand, and apply the principles presented here, you should have a 1000 to 1 edge over the person who hasn't.

Most business books fail in one or more of three ways: They're theoretical and impractical; they're general pie-in-the-sky treatments; or, they deal in nitty-gritties without revealing the fundamental principles of business success. In this book I have tried to present the fundamental principles of successful business venturing. You'll discover, in practical step-by-step fashion, how to put these principles to work for yourself. There are numerous examples showing how others have built their business ventures to guide and inspire you. Now, let's get started.

TEN BIG-PROFIT HORIZONS

There are ten broad, big-profit horizons on which you can build your fortune. The horizon that you choose to tap will depend on your desire, preference, ability, special skills, and to some extent on the capital you have available. What you've done to make a living, the businesses with which you are familiar, and the friends and acquaintances that you have may influence your choice.

These are the ten big-profit horizons:
1. Creative and technical
2. Service
3. Construction
4. Manufacturing
5. Selling
6. Trading
7. Finance
8. Rentals
9. Natural resources
10. People resources

Within each of these ten big-profit horizons there are

thousands and thousands of opportunities. Now let's look into each of these horizons.

BUILD YOUR WEALTH WITH YOUR MIND

Your mind is a boundless ocean of wealth. You can extract ideas, you can create, and you can extract stored facts and knowledge and convert these directly into large amounts of cash. Many businesses have been founded on the concept of selling mental output. All businesses have their beginnings and foundations in the mind of an entrepreneur. Here are some of the typical ways in which you can sell the output of your mind.

1. Invention
2. Consulting
3. Writing
4. Advertising ?
5. Planning
6. Research
7. Designing
8. Professional services

You'll notice that some of these activities fall into other categories that I've mentioned. There's some overlap between categories. We single out the category of the mind because it constitutes the most lucrative horizon and requires little or no cash investment to produce unusually large returns.

EARN $100 AN HOUR THIS SIMPLE WAY

Service opportunities have more than doubled during the last decade, while manufacturing work opportunities have only grown by about 15 per cent. Automation has permitted us to increase production without significantly increasing the production work force. Yet the increased produce of our highly automated industries requires service maintenance. Service is not amenable to total automation. Consequently, the opportunities in the service field have grown and the price that people are willing to pay for service has grown. The opportunities in the repair service industry are large. Here are just a few:

1. Air conditioning
2. Plumbing
3. Electrical
4. Automotive

Within each of these major categories there are numerous specialty categories. In addition, there are personal services which include:

1. Medical
2. Legal
3. Dry Cleaning
4. Pet Salons
5. Diaper services
6. Beauty and barber shops
7. Fur repair and storage
8. Reducing salons
9. Checkroom concessions
10. Pest control

There are large numbers of services that utilize the output of the mind as well as developed skills. These include:

1. Product design
2. Machine design
3. Architecture
4. Sculpture
5. Drawing and painting
6. Interior decorating
7. Public relations
8. Advertising
9. Writing

In the highly skilled service businesses, you can earn up to $100 an hour simply by directly selling the knowledge that you have or by using your knowledge to repair specialized equipment or provide specialized services. As an example, I recently had a compressor failure in one of my large air conditioners. It took the air conditioning man approximately two hours to locate the trouble and to make the replacement. His total profit on the job was $400. He made $200 an hour. Although he only billed me $100 for services, he made an additional $300 on the sale of the compressor.

You'll learn more about service businesses in Chapters Two, Three, and Four. You'll acquire sales and operating know-how in every succeeding chapter of this book.

BUILD $100,000 IN PROFITS FAST

Construction and remodeling is a lucrative business that almost anyone can enter. My friend Carl J. makes $30,000 a year doing remodeling and construction. You're especially qualified to enter this business if you have some knowledge of construction, carpentry, plumbing, air conditioning, or electrical work. You can build $100,000 in profits fast from a relatively meager start.

If you're moderately proficient as a carpenter and will take the time to study books on construction, you can get a quick and low-cost start by taking on small remodeling jobs — converting garages to extra rooms, converting basements to extra rooms, or making minor modifications to the exterior lines of houses. These jobs range in value from several hundred dollars to several thousand dollars. Land any one of these jobs to get a quick and easy start. After you get this business rolling, you can expand into basic construction. Although the construction industry goes through periodic alternations between boom and slowdown, there's always money to be made in it.

MAKE REPEAT MONEY OVER AND OVER AGAIN

A friend of mine recently entered an arena that is usually considered the sacred ground of the big bankroll investor.

He entered the manufacturing business. He started by investing $1,000 of his own money and raising additional money from other investors. He began to manufacture an electronic precipitator. In a matter of only a few months, his production and sales hit $10,000 a month, and in about a year his sales exceeded a half-million dollars. Another friend entered the manufacturing business by making footstools in his home workshop in his garage. His investment was less than $50. Within a year his venture was earning $18,000 a year. So you see, it doesn't take a lot of money to get into the manufacturing business.

The beauty of the manufacturing business lies in the fact that you earn money by doing the same thing over and over again. Consequently, you can mechanize operations and lower the cost of each step in the process. You can also use relatively unskilled labor in making your manufacturing profits. Although large companies with substantial resources dominate the manufacturing industry, there are still opportunities for small production shops to turn out products which meet one or more of the following characteristics:

1. Uncomplicated to produce (wooden wall plaques)
2. Needed in small quantities (special machine parts)
3. Needed in higher quality (fine hand-made furniture)
4. New in the result produced (a special manufacturing machine)
5. New in the way the result is produced (the sawing action of the electric knife)
6. Performs a variety of functions (multi-use tools and appliances)
7. Different in design (smaller, more attractive, etc.)
8. Less expensive
9. Individualized ("one of a kind" products)

The manufacturing business is an attractive one for any individual who has worked in industry and knows something about production. If you engage in a hobby which utilizes wood working, metalworking, foundry, or plastic molding techniques, this can provide your experience base. Manufacturing is also an attractive field for the individual who has been associated with the assembly industries — engines, machines, electronics, communications, or transportation. The horizons are unlimited. There will always be a market for the product that is different, better, or less expensive.

Chapter Six tells you how to raise capital if you don't have the cash to get into one of these bigger ventures now.

EARN $10,000 TO $100,000 A YEAR
WITHOUT INVESTING A CENT

You can earn $10,000 to $100,000 a year without investing a cent. Millions of people are doing it every year, and you can be one of them. They engage in selling. Some of them sell items that cost as little as ten cents. Others sell systems that involve millions of dollars per transaction. The small-sale seller counts on volume of sales for his profits. The big-tag seller depends on hitting an occasional sale. In either category or in the mix between, these sellers earn $10,000 to $100,000 a year.

Some sellers make an investment. *Most sellers make no investment at all.* They take a stock of items "on consignment" and pay for it from their commissions. Some salesmen feel they must invest in fine clothes, but a seller may pursue his job in khakis as well as a Hickey-Freeman suit with a diamond tie pin. Frequently, the seller in khakis outsells and outearns the man in the Hickey-Freeman suit. The atmosphere of the venture, the sophistication of the product, and the exuberance of the seller do not necessarily give an indication of the magnitude of earnings. In Chapter Eight you'll learn the secrets of sure-sell salesmen. With this information under your belt, you'll be able to launch a career in the big-profit, no-investment sales field.

PYRAMID $10 INTO $1,000 THE EASY WAY

You can "pyramid" pennies into thousands of dollars by trading to your own account in numerous and diverse fields. At the simplest level you can buy and sell appliances, furniture, bric-a-brac and antiques. You can trade in this field, too, realizing a profit on each transaction. You can engage in trading activity at a higher level of sophistication by dealing in real property or by entering the stock market or the commodity market, or by dealing in several of these markets. At every step and along every inch of the way there are profits to be earned.

Terry L. got started as a trader by buying up used window air conditioners from people who were installing central air conditioning in their homes. He bought them for $30 to $50 each and resold them for $50 to $125 per unit. He soon discovered that there were a number of heating system units of various kinds available, too. He started to buy up heating systems and extended his trade into this area as well. Within two years, he opened his own heating and air conditioning business and extended his activity to include sales and installations of new units as well.

Leslie G. of New Orleans got into the trading business by trading a boat for some used restaurant equipment. He resold and traded used restaurant equipment. In three months he had a cash profit of $2,000 and an inventory of tradeable merchandise worth another $6,000.

Frank W. played the stock market for seven years, and had a small loss at the end of that period. Most of his losses were incurred during his early years. His later years tended to decrease these losses. He got out of the market a shrewder and more cautious investor. Next he invested in real estate, and after a series of profitable trades found that he was increasing his capital 25 per cent per year. Then it looked to him as though the stock market was ready to bottom out, based on his earlier experiences in the market. He got back into the stock market, and within a year turned $10,000 into $40,000.

You'll learn all about trading and the capabilities of pyramiding $10 into $1,000, and $1,000 into $10,000, and $10,000 into $100,000, the easy way in Chapter Three.

MAKE YOUR MONEY RETURN 1,000 PER CENT

You can make your money return 1,000 per cent. How do you do it? By becoming involved in the world of finance. Recall the experience of my friend who went into the electronic precipitator business with $1,000 of his own money. He interested a number of investors who put up $1,000 each to get the business started. During the first year of operation his investors experienced a 100 per cent return on this investment. After several years, the return on their investment was 1,000 per cent. You can reap tremendous returns by making equity investments in businesses. You can also realize relatively large returns by making investments at interest in businesses and individuals. Here's how it has worked.

Milton L. went into business. He needed additional capital. He couldn't raise the capital at the bank or with usual debt financing sources, so he approached an uncle for a loan. He needed $10,000. The uncle was reluctant, so to sweeten the deal, Milt offered to repay it in monthly payments over two years at 10 per cent add-on interest plus two points to get the money. The two points on the $10,000 were worth $200, so his uncle gave him $9,800.* The uncle got interest at 10 per cent on the full $10,000 on an add-on basis. In other words, Milt makes a monthly payment, but he pays 10 per cent for two years for the full amount of $10,000. Now, let's look at this mathematically:

---

*States set maximum legal interest rates. This rate might be illegal in some states. Know your state's lending laws before you get into lending activities.

> Lender collected: 0.10 $\times$ 2 $\times$ 10,000 plus 10,000 or
>   2,000 plus 10,000 or 12,000
> Lender paid: $9,800
> That's: 2,200
> That's: 9,800 $\times$ 100% or 22% Return on Investment

Note that Milton repaid half of the $12,000 in 12 months. The lender got a good return, and Milt got the money he needed — although at relatively high cost.

If the individual needs the money desperately, it is sometimes possible to get an equity position in the business in addition to interest. Over the years, apartment houses have been financed on a debt basis, but recently there has been an increasing amount of equity participation as an essential to granting a loan. These are just a few of the many opportunities that are open to you in the world of finance. You'll learn of more in Chapter Six.

KEEP YOUR CAKE AND EAT IT TOO!

Strange as it may seem, you can keep your cake and eat it too. You can do this in the rental field. Great fortunes have been built through real estate rental. Other fortunes have grown through the rental of equipment, tools, libraries, and people, to mention only a few.

Here's how it works. You buy a rug shampoo machine with a small down payment. Then, while you pay installments, you rent the machine to users and collect a regular rental for it. The rental you collect services your debt and provides you with extra cash. You can expand your business by applying this extra cash to the purchasing of additional rug shampoo machines. Hence you retain your asset, the original machine, while collecting a regular rental on it. After a period of years the machine will be fully paid for, and then any rental that you receive for it (above the maintenance cost) will be pure profit.

This technique has built numerous fortunes in widely diverse fields of endeavor.

We mentioned "people rental;" more about that later.

DOLLARS OUT THERE — YOURS FOR THE TAKING

There are dollars out there that are yours for the taking. These dollars will flow your way if you can master the secret of tapping natural resources. The secret is not a complicated one and most people know it, yet very few people know how to tap it.

Natural resources are the raw materials that feed our modern way of life. There's money to be made in utilizing these natural resources and in disposing of the waste that is generated in their utilization. There's wealth under the earth, on the earth, and in the sky above the earth. This wealth consists of precious minerals, fossil fuels, land, location of the land, scenery and the natural resources of the land including forests, crops, water, and life on the land and within the waters, and air space above the land.

Natural resources provide recreation and pleasure and provide opportunities to tap the boating, fishing, surfing, swimming, travel, and other markets. The use of these natural resources results in scrap. Somebody has to dispose of the scrap. There are large profits to be made in salvage, too. We'll say more about these possibilities in succeeding chapters.

PEOPLE WANT TO MAKE BIG MONEY FOR YOU

You want to make money — so do other people. You're more astute than most and consequently you are going to make your money by engaging in your own business. Many others who want to make money will prefer to do so by working for someone else — you. Big money is made by selling "human resources" at a profit. Human resources are required in both manufacturing and service businesses. But the direct "sale" of human resources provides additional areas for profitable business. You can make money by "selling" people resources in any of several businesses:

1. Employment agency
2. Temporary help agency
3. Actor's or artist's agency
4. Contract job shop

These are only a few of the opportunities open to you, because other people want to make money and consequently will share some of what you help them get with you in return for your service.

HOW 75 CENTS LAUNCHED A BUSINESS

Harry K., mentioned earlier in this chapter, launched a new career with 75 cents! How? Simple for Harry. He scanned classified ads with a passion. This one caught his eye:

Magic Car Wash Detergent. Retail $1.95.
Dozen $6.00. Sample 75¢.

He sent 75 cents, demonstrated the sample to several neighbors, and got four orders with deposits. From there he went to wholesaling the detergent to filling stations for $12 a dozen. He added other specialty items and accessories to his line, and built his business to $25,000 a year profit.

In case you're wondering about how Blaine U. built $75 into a $100,000 a year business, I'd like to point out that he's only one of many who've done it with knowledge and technology. He developed a system for keeping inventory status in a business. The model cost him $75 to make. He used the model to demonstrate, sell, and take orders. The first ten systems that he sold developed enough referral business to get his electronics firm going in a big way.

NOW GET WITH IT

In this chapter we've shown you the ten big profit horizons and a few of the ways you can tap them to make your fortune. Now it's up to you. If you want to become fantastically rich; if you want to become independent; if you want to minimize the risk that it takes to get into business, then read further. But do more than read. Study. Plan. Scheme. Work at it. If you'll do these things, you'll be rich beyond your wildest dreams in a matter of one to three years. You don't need a lot of money to start. You don't have to work yourself to death — you can even do it in just a little of your spare time. Before you know it, you'll be financially independent and command a large income.

Chapter 2

MONEYMAKING BUSINESSES
THAT YOU CAN START WITH
$20 OR LESS

TWENTY BUCKS BUYS A LOT!

There's an almost infinite variety of businesses that you can get into with $20 or less by working the business from your home. Twenty bucks will buy a lot in the way of raw materials, tools, and information. While this amount of money doesn't look like much to the man with a fat budget, the resourceful man can do an awful lot with it. And that's what this chapter is about. Just to get a feel for what $20 will do, here are a few of the things that $20 will buy:

1. Enough lumber to build a $200 piece of furniture.
2. A used piece of furniture that you can refinish and sell for $200.
3. An antique that you can resell for $100.
4. A rare book or coin that you can resell for from $50 to $100.
5. Enough material to make $500 worth of jewelry.

6. Enough gasoline to collect $250 for deliveries.
7. Enough paper to convert into $100 worth of mimeographing.
8. Drawing instruments that will make you thousands of dollars.
9. The basic equipment for a janitorial service.
10. Hand tools for a repair service.

The possibilities are endless. Here are a few more ideas to help you appreciate the power of a $20 bill:

1. Enough groceries to manufacture $60 worth of pies and cakes.
2. Purchase or down payment on a registered animal for breeding purposes.
3. Used typewriter for secretarial service or envelope addressing service.
4. Enough raw popcorn to resell for $60 to $80.
5. Enough chemicals to earn $500 in fire extinguisher service.
6. A used lawnmower that will earn hundreds of dollars in lawn mowing fees.
7. Down payment on a rubber stamp-making machine.
8. Enough chemicals to make $200 worth of perfume.
9. A down payment for a course on almost any skill you wish to learn.
10. Sample kits that open the door to thousands of dollars in sales.

So you see, a $20 bill will buy quite a bit in the way of used merchandise that can be reconditioned and sold at a higher value, raw materials that can be converted into expensive end products, tools and equipment that can be used to make a considerable amount of money in a service business, or an education which can be applied to earn larger amounts of money than you are now accustomed to earning. If I may say so again, this list is not all-inclusive, and if you'll put your thinking cap on, you'll come up with many additional possibilities. The point is that a $20 bill gives you a considerable amount of capability (especially when you take stock of what else you may have), and it seems like a lot more when you look at it in light of these examples.

WHAT ELSE HAVE YOU GOT?

You have numerous resources that you can harness in establishing your own business right in your own home. Here is a list of some of the tools, appliances, and equipment you may possess which can be put to work in a home business to get you started in a big-time business venture career:

Hand tools
Power tools
Lawn mower
Automobile
Kitchen equipment
Silver and china
Sewing machine
Garden tools
Typewriter
Washing machine
Floor buffer
Sports equipment
Adding machine

In addition to these devices, which can be used as production implements, teaching devices, service business equipment or even as rental items, you probably have a garage, a basement, or a spare room that you can use as an office, factory, or a warehouse. Furthermore, if you'll dig through the attic, the basement, and the garage, you'll probably find lots of things that can be repaired or upgraded and sold for cash. You'll probably find some things that still work, but that you don't need. They can be resold as they are. Even unrepairable junk has some scrap value. Hence, you can come up with additional cash to launch your own business.

You have other resources in the form of cash, assets that can be converted into cash, or assets that can be used as collateral for a loan. Here are just a few:

1. Equity in your home
2. Stocks and bonds
3. Furniture
4. Insurance policies
5. Jewelry
6. Equity in automobiles
7. Equity in other properties

With these assets you can raise additional capital to supplement that $20 bill if you wish. Frankly, I think it is a good idea to start with as little as possible. Although your chances of success are usually better with a larger amount of money, I prefer the route of starting a business on a small amount of money while you are still gainfully employed. Thus you learn more about conducting a business with less risk. Then, when you put bigger chips into the game, your chances of success are greatly enhanced. More about raising larger amounts of capital in Chapter Six.

TEN BUSINESSES THAT WERE STARTED WITH $20 OR LESS

Mike J. was a low-paid clerk in a large Midwestern manufacturing company. For years he sat at his desk watching others — no better, or smarter, or harder working — advance in salary and position while he toiled, struggling to make ends meet, in a dreary dead-end job. Finally, one day, he decided to strike out in his own spare-time business. Using the knowledge gained on his job, he bought a small adding machine — for practically nothing — and started his own accounting business. This business had a special built-in "reward" feature that made clients call him day and night (convenient on-the-premises service) — and his income suddenly leaped from

$5,000 to $10,000. At $15,000, with more business than he could handle, he opened up offices with full-time help, and quit his clerk's job (tearing his time-card to little pieces and throwing it in his boss's face). Today, John P. is in the $50,000 a year tax bracket, with an automatic income (others do most of the work) from a business he supervises just TWO DAYS a week — with ample time left for sunny vacations, golfing, yachting, or lounging around his $100,000 house, with a built-in swimming pool and two Cadillacs in the driveway.

Joe S. was a salaried TV repairman with a large TV sales and service organization, making only $125 a week — with a wife, 3 children, a car and mortgage payments. He started to study industrial electronics with books that he borrowed at the public library. After six months of study, he felt that he understood industrial electronic equipment well enough to start servicing it. With a $20 investment, he purchased letter-heads and postage and sent letters to the maintenance supervisors of the industrial plants in his area. Within a year, he was making $5,000 in his spare time. After two years, his business had grown to such an extent that he had to quit his TV servicing job in order to handle his own industrial business.

Thurston F. was a production worker in a large manufacturing plant till he was laid off. He had always had a desire to go into business for himself, but didn't quite know how to do it. One day, while he was with his children at a carnival, he noticed that the "Ices" that his kids paid 20¢ for were nothing but granulated ice and half a penny's worth of syrup. Thurston immediately bought himself an ice-grinding machine and a syrup dispenser and traveled to festivals, carnivals, and other affairs with his machine. He made $5,000 the first year.

Mary L., a secretary and a widow, had three children to raise. Her budget was pressed and she had a hard time making ends meet with the salary she was earning. She established a secretarial service. She mimeographed a form letter and sent it to churches, clubs, civic organizations, and small businesses that ordinarily do not have full-time secretarial help.

Her business grew rapidly. Within three months, all of the girls in her office were moonlight employees of Mary's. Within six months she quit her job to devote full time to her secretarial service.

Joe B. was an office manager. He decided to start his own janitorial service venture. He contacted several building owners and eventually got a contract for a building. Each night he and two of his grown children went into the building and cleaned it up. The owner of the building was so satisfied with Joe's service that he offered him the maintenance contracts on several other buildings.

Martin L. was laid off during a business recession and found jobs scarce. Instead of taking the time during which he drew unemployment compensation to look for another job in a market where jobs were virtually unfindable, Martin decided to start his own business. He knew something about electroplating, and he decided that a logical business for him to get into would be manufacturing plated accessories for men and women's clothing and jewelry. He made a number of samples and then called on the salesmen who worked at the plant at which he was employed. One of the salesmen referred him to a friend who called on accounts that bought this type of merchandise. This referral resulted in sales of $30,000 the first year. Needless to say, Martin L. made it.

Miles S. was a chemist for a large corporation. He noticed that a number of companies had become successful by selling detergents and soap products through sales organizations. He decided to manufacture soap products in his garage at night. The chemicals for his original batch cost $10, but he sold the batch for $75. After two months of operation, his business was earning about $250 a month for him after salesman's commissions. He decided to quit his job immediately, borrow the capital, and expand his business. Today Miles S. has an organization with sales in excess of $1,000,000 a year.

William S. was another man who got caught in a layoff. He decided to open a "Trade Mart." He found an old warehouse that he could rent for $200 a month. He convinced the owner of the warehouse that he'd make his venture pay off and therefore was able to move in without paying any rent at all. He invested in two ads, each of which cost him $5. One of the ads advertised a gigantic sale at which all kinds of bargains could be found. He placed that ad under "Miscellaneous Goods For Sale." He placed another ad under "Business Opportunities," and advertised sales spaces for rent in the big Trade Mart. On his opening day, he had fifteen booths rented at $5 a day. After thirty days, he had thirty booths rented. Some of his tenants rent their spaces for only a few days; others rent them on a continuing basis. The annual turnover of goods in his Trade Mart approaches $1,000,000, and business is picking up as antique dealers and art dealers are beginning to gravitate to his Trade Mart.

Hogart V. was a retail clerk in a ladies' ready-to-wear store. His hobby was art, and he found himself sketching dress designs in his spare time. He showed some of his designs to a salesman for a small dress factory. The salesman asked if he could take the designs along to show his boss. On his next visit he commissioned Hogart to design some dresses. The dresses became high-volume sellers and Hogart was soon earning more money from his design activities than he was as a retail clerk.

Jim J. is a pharmacist. He was employed by a large drug store chain but was anxious to get into business for himself. He decided to conduct a systematic investigation of drug stores in the state that were owned by older men who might be reaching retirement age. He finally located a store within thirty miles of his home that was for sale. He went to see the aged owner, and told him that he had no money to invest but that he was willing to go to work on a salary till he earned enough money to make the down payment to buy the drug store. They made a deal; today Jim owns the drug store.

Note that in each of these starts, the entrepreneur did one or more of the following things:

1. Used a skill he already possessed
2. Expanded a skill he already possessed
3. Started his business while still gainfully employed
4. Was forced into accomplishing something fast because he didn't have a job
5. Took a creative approach to start his business
6. Used resources (other than cash) which he had available
7. Bargained to avoid an outlay of cash at the start
8. Employed special skills where they were needed
9. Put a dedicated effort into starting and running his business
10. Utilized business contacts that he already had established

SERVICE BUSINESSES THAT YOU CAN START FOR $20 OR LESS

Service businesses offer the best opportunities for low dollar investment starts. This is so because you can operate the businesses from your home, using tools and other forms of capital equipment that you already have available. Furthermore, you can provide the services either during the day or during the evening. Evening service is often preferable, since in many families no one is at home during the day. Here are some of the service businesses that you can start for $20 or less:

Property management
Library research and abstracting
Accounting and bookkeeping
Dancing instruction
Office machine repair
Secretarial service
Addressing service
Advertising, copywriting and art
Photography

Air conditioning repairs
Delivery service
Animal grooming
Janitorial services
Laundry and ironing service
Musical instrument instruction
Catering
Home repairs
Design services
Product development
Shoe repair service
Wedding service
Business consulting
Writing
Plumbing
Radio-TV repair
Child care
Antique restoration
Newspaper clipping service
Vending machine route service
Public relations
Sales promotion
Duplicating service
Entertainment agency

This only scratches the surface of the infinite possibilities that are open to you in the service business.

RETAIL/MAIL ORDER BUSINESSES
FOR SHOESTRING STARTS

You can get off to a low-cost start in retail and mail order by operating your business from your home. If you're retailing, you can conduct your business through parties that you give in the homes of other people or in your own home. You can establish regular hours during which you'll be open if you wish or you can be open an infinite number of hours in the old "Mom and Pop" grocery store style. However, be sure to check the zoning in your city. Some cities have zoning laws which prevent the conduct of a business from a residence. If this is the case, you'll have to switch to mail order and telephone selling. Mail order and telephone selling offer numerous opportunities for the individual who wants to go into business for himself. Here are just a few of the many businesses in retail and mail order that you can start for very little cash:

Dress, suit, shoe and other clothing sales
China, silver, and kitchenware sales
Radio, TV, and appliance sales
New and used office machine sales
Automobile sales
Insurance, real estate, and other intangible sales
Sporting and athletic equipment sales
Correspondence course sales
Book sales
Cosmetic and sundry drug sales
Sale of homemade products and handicrafts
Greeting card sales
Jewelry, watch, and clock sales
Marine equipment sales
Doll and toy sales
Home accessory sales
Gadget sales
Import-export sales

Almost anything that can be sold in the normal retail store can be sold by telephone or by mail. In addition to selling by mail or retailing from your home, you can sell through salesmen on a commission basis. Some of your friends may get interested in the products that you are selling and may be willing to sell for you on a commission. You can start these businesses for $20 or less if you sell from a sample and deliver later or sell by mail.

MANUFACTURING BUSINESSES THAT
$20 WILL START

Most manufacturing businesses require more than $20 to start. However, there are some manufacturing businesses which can be started on a small scale, such as home manufacturing businesses. In the selection matrix in Chapter Five you'll learn that a manufacturing business that is limited in nature may be started for as little as $10. Here are some of the products that you can manufacture in a garage, basement, kitchen, or spare room with $20 or less starting capital:

Soaps and detergents
Adhesives
Cosmetics
Cakes and pies
Antique reproductions
Electronic devices
Burglar alarms
Crating
Belts and other leather goods
Jewelry
Dress Accessories
Rubber stamps
Towel racks
Sample cases
Special tools
Furniture
Clothing
Drapes
Ceramics
Store fixtures
Utility trailers
Boats and marine equipment
Neckties
Books (printing)
Sports equipment (e.g., fish lures)

A single product cited in some of these ventures might cost considerably more than $20. However, if you had a reputation as a builder of boats, for example, you might sell on the basis of a sketch and specifications and get an advance against the order that would permit you to buy the materials to build your first boat. The same holds true for utility trailers and other large or specialized items. When you custom manufacture, you get a deposit on the product before you start to make it. Be sure to get a signed contract so you'll have legal recourse in case the buyer tries to back out.

CASH IN ON A FABULOUS DIRECT SELLING FORTUNE

Direct selling is a business that you can get into without investing in more than a postage stamp or two. There is a legion of direct salesmen who sell from door-to-door, to businesses, and to friends without carrying any inventory or making any investment whatsoever. They sell either from samples provided by the manufacturer or from catalogs and other sales aids provided by the manufacturer. These salesmen take orders and then have the orders filled directly from the factory, or they consolidate their orders and make deliveries themselves. Direct salesmen sell everything from shoelaces to house trailers and boats. Their earnings range from a few thousand dollars a year for part-timers to $50,000 and even $100,000 for aggressive sellers of big-ticket items. Their commissions on their sales are generally greater than commissions that are paid to employee salesmen. They're in business for themselves, and their earnings are limited only by their own initiatives.

There are a number of publications catering to the direct selling fraternity. Two of these are:

Specialty Salesman
307 N. Michigan Avenue
Chicago, Illinois 60601

Salesman's Opportunity
850 N. Dearborn Street
Chicago, Illinois 60610

Additional sources for direct sales opportunities can be found through Thomas' Directory, which you can find in your public library. You'll find Chapter Eight especially interesting and instructive if you want to enter the field of direct sales.

Another opportunity that presents itself in the field of direct sales is the opportunity to build a pyramid organization. Here's how it works:

You sign up as a salesman of the product. You start to sell, develop your selling techniques and build your own selling record. Then you recruit salesmen who work for you and you get a percentage of their earnings. They are *your* commissioned employees rather than direct employees of the manufacturer. If you can develop a good enough sales record and if the manufacturer that you are buying from is a small enough manufacturer, he will, in some instances, give you protected territory and permit you to build your own sales organization within it. There are a number of pyramid type sales organization set-ups in existence at the present time. One of the outstanding examples of a successful pyramid sales organization is Amway.

A $20 BILL CAN BECOME A $1000 BUSINESS START

Small amounts of money can be used to start businesses requiring relatively large amounts of borrowed capital. The principle of using a small amount of your own money and borrowing a large amount of money for investment purposes is known as leverage. Leverage works this way: Suppose you have $20 in cash to start. You need $1000 in order to get your business going. You go to your banker and ask him to lend you $300 on a signature loan. We will assume that your financial statement is good enough to warrant this amount of loan. (You'll learn how to prepare a financial statement and other facets of raising capital in Chapter Six.) Then you have the initial $20 plus the $300 that you borrowed. Assuming that you need four pieces of equipment that cost $250 each and can arrange to buy them for $50 down, you take $200 out of your initial $320 to make the down payment. Hence you have $1000 worth of equipment and $120 in operating cash.

In the process of leveraging you have acquired a total of $1100 in debts. You have equity in equipment and cash to show for the debt that you've incurred. This equipment and your operating capital of $120 enables you to earn the money to service the debt on the equipment as well as the debt that you incurred with your signature loan. There is a danger in high leverage in that the business must have sales in excess of expenses and debt payments. Many new business starts turn into failures because the cash flow is inadequate to service the debt because sales are too low or expenses too high, or both. When this occurs the equipment is repossessed and you're in the position of being a poor credit risk when you undertake new and future ventures.

CAPTURE A $1000 PROFIT OPPORTUNITY WITH $20

There are several ways in which you can capture $1000 and larger profit opportunities with amounts of money as small as $20 or less. There won't be too many times during your lifetime when you can take advantage of some of these techniques to realize large profit opportunities with such a small amount of money. Some of the mechanisms for doing this are:

1. Options
2. Down payments
3. Deposits

4. Advertisements
5. Investments in undervalued stocks and bonds
6. Discount purchase of notes

Here's how they work:

John Adler met Thomas Allen, who was looking for a small factory location. John searched for and located a suitable property. He found that the property could be purchased for less money than Mr. Allen was willing to pay. John got a ten-day option from the seller for $20 because the property was located in a small "dead" town. John drew up a written agreement and Mr. Allen agreed to sign it. John then revealed the location of his property. He showed Mr. Allen the property, quoting a price that included a nice profit for himself, and Mr. Allen bought it. There's some danger that this kind of deal can fall through if your prospective buyer waits till your option lapses and then contacts the seller directly. However, John protected himself against this contingency by making a written agreement with Mr. Allen before exposing the property to him.

Down payments or deposits on property work in much the same way as an option. But be careful that you don't enter into a contract which makes you liable for more than the amount of the deposit, in case you have to forfeit it.

An investment of $20 or less in advertisements can frequently turn large profits for you. Here's how it works: You locate a property or merchandise that is available for sale. You advertise the merchandise for sale at a price that includes your profit. Then, when you make the deal to sell the merchandise, you go back to the seller and negotiate a line of credit with him. Or, if you have solid contracts, you can borrow the cash to make the purchase.

People have often borrowed cash from an individual and signed promissory notes. If a noteholder is strapped for cash, he'll sometimes sell these notes for as low as 40 per cent of the unpaid balance in the case of a first lien note, or as low as 25 per cent in the case of a second lien. If your credit is good, you can borrow the money to buy such a note. You collect the full amount of the note plus interest, and if the lender defaults, you get the property.

HOW $20 GREW TO $100 IN THREE HOURS

Gary S. walked into a ceramic shop that was going out of business. The proprietor had sold most of the merchandise and had just a few pieces left. Gary asked the proprietor what he'd take for the remainder, and he quoted $50. Gary said, "Well, I've only got $20," and laid the $20 bill on the counter. "Sold!" said the proprietor, and Gary loaded the merchandise into his car. He took it to a downtown furniture store and offered it for sale for $100. He sold it immediately and in less than three hours had converted a $20 bill into $100.

This is an instance of the fortunate low, low buy. Opportunities of this kind present themselves from time to time in connection with both new and used merchandise. You sometimes bump into an opportunity where you actually don't have to invest a penny in cash as a result of some other deal that you've made. For example, houses or commercial property that I've purchased sometimes contained discarded items that had salvage value. In one instance, the salvage value of the abandoned items came to about $500. Always look for side opportunities of this kind whenever you make a deal.

LAUNCH A NEW CAREER WITH $20

So you see, $20 is quite a lot of money, and you can perform miracles with it either directly or by using the $20 as leverage for larger amounts of money. The businesses that you can most readily enter with such a small nest egg include service businesses, trading activities, small home business manufacturing activities, creative and technical activities, and direct or limited sales activities. In most instances, a $20 start is best made while you're still gainfully employed. Such a limited amount of capital makes you too vulnerable to be a full-time "starter." Many small businesses started on a moonlight basis continue as moonlight activities for long periods of time, but probably 25 per cent of the businesses started as moonlight and home activities turn into full-time activities for the entrepreneur in a few years.

The profits you can make, the success you can achieve, and the growth you can experience from a low dollar start is limited only by yourself. If you have the optimism, the desire, the stamina, and the determination to make your $20 start a successful one, you can do it, just as many others have.

Chapter 3

MAKE THOUSANDS FAST WITH A $500 START

A $500 START GIVES YOU A BIG ADVANTAGE

If you have $500 with which to start your business, you can start any of the businesses discussed earlier on a larger and more secure scale. In addition, you can enter a larger business and tap many additional opportunities which you couldn't enter with a $20 start. Furthermore, by leveraging your $500, you can obtain $5,000 or more to start your business on an even larger scale.

SEND UP A TRIAL BALLOON

I do not subscribe to the myth that experience is the best teacher. I think experience is an excellent teacher, but investigation, study, and planning are a smarter way to work than to rely totally on experience. However, it's a good idea to take advantage of lessons that can be gained by setting up trial experiences. This can be done with very low risk. Send up a "trial balloon" on your business by using only a small amount of your $500 as a start.

If you are going to sell TV sets, get one sample and back this with a catalog for selling. If you're going to manufacture an electronic precipitator to reduce air pollution, build a small, inexpensive model before you build a full-scale prototype. If you're going into the mail order business, try small mailings of different, coded copy before you select copy for a big printing and mailing. A trial balloon is a cheap test. Moonlighting is another approach to trial ballooning. You maintain the security that you may have as the result of a job. Thus the trial balloon enables you to learn to work more efficiently with bigger dollars. You minimize risk, and when you put all of your money to work, you'll reap bigger, surer profits as a result of the experience that you have gained by working with smaller capital.

ONE-TIME PROFIT VENTURES THAT YOU CAN START WITH $500 OR LESS

There are some one-shot activities and business opportunities that you can capitalize on with $500 or less. In some instances these one-time opportunities can be repeated and can be turned into continuing businesses. In most cases, though, they're one-shot — a deal at a time. This strategy is particularly productive if you simply want to build some spare income and have no intention of ever leaving your main employment.

Most one-shot opportunities involve a buy and sell or trade type of deal, so let's take a look at the ways in which you can exploit buy and sell or trade opportunities.

The trader's best friend is the classified section of newspapers and other periodicals, which offer new and used merchandise for sale and contain offers to buy.

The basic technique in using the classifieds to exploit

one-time opportunities is to look for merchandise or property for sale. Buy it and then turn around and sell the merchandise or property. You can sell through personal contact, telephone contact, or by placing a for sale ad. The name of the game is to sell for more than you paid.

To get a feel for the possibilities, let's take a look at some of the classifications in a typical newspaper classified section:

Births: Nothing you can buy here but if you're selling a product or service for the baby market, this is a good place to find leads.

Personal Ads and Business Personal Ads: One of these ads offers oil portraits hand-painted from snapshots. This is not a one-shot opportunity, but it might very well turn into a selling or sales opportunity.

Transportation and Mobile Homes: This includes antique cars, automobiles of all makes and descriptions, trucks, trailers, campers, mobile homes, motorcycles, and motorbikes. There are opportunities here to buy and sell at a profit. To explore these opportunities, simply get on the telephone. Start making calls to try to unearth a good buy.

Sports, Resorts, and Travel: You'll spot many leads in these ads. Again, just start phoning.

Business Opportunities: A listing of retail stores, franchise distributorships, restaurants and lounges, service businesses, hotels and motels, manufacturing and wholesale businesses, and newspaper print shops for sale. This category is particularly productive of one-time deals that can be made with as little as $500 down. If you find a good buy under this category, you can turn it around and sell it at a profit. One caution here: If you buy a business or a property with the down payment, the debt has to be serviced. You've got to make the monthly payments till you sell the property. Here, too, you can take advantage of option opportunities, which we discussed elsewhere.

Partnerships Wanted: Sometimes a money bonanza. You may find a situation here that you may want to enter yourself, or you may want to play the role of "finder" for the person who is looking for a partner.

Help Wanted and Positions Wanted: You can play the role of finder and collect a finder's fee in some instances.

Instruction and Education: Consider any special knowledge or skills you can teach. Think also of selling the teaching or tutoring skills of others.

Money to Loan, Money Wanted, Mortgages, Stocks and Bonds: There are numerous finder's fee opportunities under this category, and you may find sources of capital for your own ventures here.

Livestock, Pets, and Poultry: This is an area that offers buy and sell or trade opportunities if you're particularly fond of and know animals. I know a lady in her eighties who makes a living buying and selling dogs through the classified ads.

Merchandise For Sale: Includes "Miscellaneous," "Boats and Motors," "Cameras and Supplies," "Books, Coins, and Stamps," "Art Goods," "Antiques," "Jewelry, Watches, Diamonds," "Household Furniture," "Pianos and Musical Instruments," "Appliances," "Building Materials," "Heating and Air Conditioning Equipment," "Cafe and Bar Fixtures," "Showcases, Store Fixtures," "Office Furniture and Equipment," "Farm Equipment," "Machinery and Supplies," "Wearing Apparel," and other items. This area is obviously rich in buy and sell or trade opportunities.

Real Estate: Includes "Rental Property," "Property For Sale," "Property Wanted," "Residential, Single," "Residential, Multiple," "Commercial," "Warehousing," "Offices," and "Raw Land." Again, this is a lucrative trading area. There are finding, leasing, and buy and sell opportunities.

While this run through the classified section may seem elementary, I think it is productive in highlighting the vast array of opportunities that land on your doorstep every morning in the classified section of your newspaper. In exploring these opportunities, use the following procedure:

1. Scan the ads for apparent bargains
2. Circle ads that look interesting
3. Make preliminary telephone call investigation
4. Keep notes on your telephone calls
5. Eliminate the less promising potentials
6. Take the promising potentials and either call back or make a personal visit to determine the true quality of the deal.

If you study the ads on a regular basis, watch for continuing repeats. The more often an ad is repeated, the lower the price is likely to get. Some of the nuisances that you will encounter in this activity include dealers who place come-on ads for their merchandise, unavailability of the seller which requires replacing calls at a later time, and occasional trips to look at merchandise that is already sold when you arrive.

The classifieds are not necessarily "one-time" profit opportunities, and are not the only avenue for exploiting one-time profit ventures. You may come across a good buy during a trip downtown, during a visit with a friend, or during the course of your daily work activity. If you trade actively on a regular basis and have an established place of business, opportunities will frequently be brought to you. Other sources of one-time buy opportunities include the foreclosure bulleting board at the county court house, legal notices concerning divorces and estate sales, and news of major building remodeling programs.

The big disadvantage of one-time ventures is that the time spent in the venture is not necessarily productive of repeat opportunities. So let's take a look at businesses that you can start with $500 or less that do have repeat business potential.

BUSINESSES THAT YOU CAN
START WITH $500 OR LESS

You can obviously start any of the $20 start businesses

discussed in the preceding chapter with more money. However, you can start them on a considerably larger scale. In some instances, a bigger start kitty will enable you to start immediately on a full-time basis without relying on income from a full-time job. Now let's look at some of the additional possibilities that open up when you have $500 available for a start.

Your present work can lead you into an investment opportunity that will make a fortune. George W. was purchasing agent for a printing firm. One of his paper supplier's salesmen told him about an idea he had for a paper-cutting machine design. The salesman had invested a considerable amount of money in building a model, but needed $350 to complete it. George offered to provide the $350 for 10 per cent equity (10 per cent ownership) in the invention. They completed the machine and licensed the design to a manufacturer. George's income from a $350 investment exceeds $5,000 a year. This was essentially a technical man-investor partnership. Another possible combination is a talent-talent partnership where one partner is the technical man and the other is strong in sales.

Opportunities in all fields are open to you with a $500 start, because with $500 you can either work from your home or set up a downtown office from which to work. With $500 you can capitalize more fully on your creative output because you can carry the idea through to the product stage. For example, I have a friend who is a writer. He publishes his own output for extra profit. If you're a musician, you can form a band or start an entertainment agency.

During the past two decades, many electronics companies have been started with $500 or less. If you want to enter the interior decorating business, a service requiring creative ability, you can increase your profits by stocking some of your own merchandise and producing some of your own drapes, for example.

Precision servicing businesses, such as custom foreign car repairs or electronic equipment servicing, which require expensive equipment, are open to you with a $500 starting budget. A $500 start in any business enables you to start in a down town location where you can benefit from greater traffic, greater sales and faster profit.

Five hundred dollars enables you to enter the remodeling field. Interior remodeling and redecorating, garage and basement conversions, minor exterior conversions, and the construction of garages and out-house buildings are also open to you. It's difficult to start this business with less than $500 in assets because of the equipment requirements.

Your start in manufacturing can be more realistic with a $500 start. You're able to buy more adequate equipment, manufacture larger production runs, and take advantage of quantity buying. You also have advantages in terms of being able to spend more to foster the sale of your products.

In trading, a $500 start enables you to work in larger units. It enables you to get into wholesale as well as retail trading. One of my friends makes a killing by trading electronic test equipment and stereos.

Milton K. got into the rental business. He leased a large amount of retail space at a wholesale price. Then he subleased small portions of the space at higher rental rates to a number of tenants. I got into the rentals business by using $500 as a down payment on a house that I then rented for $150 a month. The payments I had to make were only $100 a month, so I had all of my money back in ten months.

The rental business embraces a larger horizon than the rental of real estate. With $500 you can buy equipment which can be rented at substantial profits. Almost anything that you can think of is being rented these days. The basic principle to apply in getting into the equipment and general product rental business is to buy all of your purchases on time payments. Roland H. used $500 for down payments on $5,000 worth of rentable merchandise. Another tactic to employ here is to buy *used* equipment. If you buy good but used items for 10 to 30 per cent cost of new, you'll have additional leverage in terms of cost over the leverage you'll get from buying on time. Although you might have more maintenance costs to pay on your used equipment, you can end up with equipment valued at $10,000 to $50,000 "new" with an actual cash investment of only $500. Of course, as in real estate rentals, the rents have to be sufficient to service the debt and provide a cash flow.

You can invest in and profit on *natural resources* with a $500 start by leasing and operating a farm, by investing in an oil syndicate, by buying stocks in natural resource companies, through mineral right leases, and through your own explorations. These areas are highly specialized ones, and if you have interests in this direction, I suggest you tap additional reference sources.

HEDGE TO MINIMIZE CHANCE

You should "hedge" your investments to minimize the chances that you take. A common "hedging" technique is to buy and sell simultaneously, or almost simultaneously, for delivery at some future date. You buy and sell at the same time to avoid losses due to price fluctuation. For example, a dealer has bought 10,000 bushels of wheat, which he will sell in thirty days. If the price of wheat goes up in that period, the seller earns his normal profit plus the price increase. But, if the price of wheat goes down, the dealer's income is reduced.

The dealer will want to profit on the conversion, not speculate on commodity price fluctuations. To protect himself, he sells 10,000 bushels short* for delivery in thirty days. The dealer then buys to cover the short after 30 days. If

---

*Short — to sell a commodity, stock, or merchandise which you do not own. You borrow whatever you sell short and you must replace it at a later date.

the price goes down, the profit on this transaction covers the loss due to the decrease in price of the wheat he originally bought for re-sale.

There are some business techniques that provide "hedges" that are not consistent with this classical interpretation. For example, diversification can be regarded as a hedge against seasonal business or business changes in narrow markets. A boat dealer whose spring and summer sales were great boosted his winter business by diversifying into snowmobiles. If your business is dependent on one segment of the community, diversify by getting into an additional business that caters to another segment of the community. A hardware dealer who had the contractor business in his town suffered whenever building activity was down. He added kitchenware to bring housewives and new business into his store during those times.

TURN $500 INTO THOUSANDS
IN AS LITTLE AS ONE MONTH

You can turn $500 into large amounts of money very quickly and obtain a going business in the process. This big money growth strategy is based on purchasing an existing business. The business may be available for purchase for one of the following reasons:

1. Owner's age
2. Owner's health
3. Owner's disinterest
4. Owner's family situation
5. Unprofitable
6. Forced to relocate
7. Failure or bankruptcy

Any of these reasons may cause an owner to want to sell his business. If the business is a going, profitable business, you'll hardly buy it for as little as $500. However, $500 may open the door either as a down payment or as seed money augmented by a loan. If the business is small enough or unprofitable, it is possible that you can purchase the business for as little as $500. In either event, if you can purchase the assets of a business for less than their value, or if you can purchase a going business for as little as one to three years' profits, there's considerable merit in giving the situation consideration.

If you buy a business that is going poorly or is forced to relocate and buy the assets only for considerably less than book value, you can sell off some of the assets to pull immediate cash. In many instances the buyer has recouped several times what he has paid for the business in a matter of a month or two. If you purchase a going business, there is still a possibility that you can "pull cash" by selling off some of the capital equipment which may actually not be needed in the business. Hence you can end up with all or more than you have originally spent and still have a going business to provide you with an automatic, steady income.

Some things to bear in mind when purchasing a business: Either purchase the assets only and be sure that you can get free title to them or, if you purchase the business as an entity, be sure that there aren't a host of liabilities that can clobber you in the process. It's a good idea to work through a lawyer in purchasing a business to protect yourself against such eventualities. If there's real estate involved in the purchase, be sure that you're getting title to the property clear to the amount of debt that you think you're assuming.

SMALL CHIPS BECOME MULTI-MILLION DOLLAR BUSINESSES

At the age of twenty-six, Clarence Birdseye went to Labrador. With some shrewd trading, he quickly turned a profit of $6,000. During this venture, he noticed that animals and foods that froze quickly retained their natural consistency, while slow freezing made the meat and foods grainy due to the formation of large ice crystals. When he returned to the United States he worked in the corner of a large ice cream plant in New Jersey, developing his quick-freeze process. In 1923 he organized a company and put quick-frozen fish on the market, but soon went broke. Later, using his insurance as collateral, he got up enough money to design a better freezer and to form a new company. He got additional financial backing and just six years later, in 1929, he sold his company for $22,000,000.

I'm sure you're familiar with Life Savers. The inventor of Life Savers, Clarence Crane, a Cleveland candy maker, sold his company for so little money that you could have made the down payment with $500. Here's what happened: Edward J. Noble worked his way through Yale selling books and trolley car ads. He tried Life Savers and liked them, so he went to see the inventor, Clarence Crane, to sell him some trolley advertising.

Noble got interested in Life Savers and ended up buying the business for a few thousand dollars. At the time Life Savers were not going over too well, because the tubes that the Life Savers were packed in were a problem — the tubes were glued and glue taste got through to the Life Savers. The tubes were so stiff that customers tended to break their fingernails in trying to open them. Noble's solution was to wrap the mints in foil and then place the paper wrapping which required glue over the foil. Noble became a multimillionaire, and the rest of the Life Saver story is history.

TREMENDOUS PROFITS IN FIFTEEN DAYS

Clara N. started a business from scratch and began earning a profit in fifteen days. How did she do it? She employed a novel concept in conjunction with a rather regular and ordinary business. She started a sewing center, but her sewing center was different. Her's was a lingerie sewing center. She came upon the idea when a friend who worked in a lingerie factory told her that lingerie remnant material was available at one or two dollars a yard. She purchased some of the material and developed techniques for making beautiful lingerie. She was so impressed with the results of her handi-work that she decided to open a lingerie sewing center. She leased a building and stocked it with the remnant lingerie material and the lace and trim that is used in making lingerie. She acquired a line of sewing machines and then started running classified ads under "Personals" in the newspaper that read: "Ladies, learn to sew lovely lingerie." She gave courses, consisting of approximately ten hours of instruction, for $30. Her classes filled, her business boomed, and her material sales skyrocketed. She sold as many sewing machines as some of her established competitors. Just fifteen days after she opened her doors for business she was turning a tidy profit, and she made $12,000 profit during her first year of business.

YOUR BUDGET IS A KEY FACTOR

Your family's subsistence budget is a key factor to con-sider in deciding whether to start your business as a home business or whether to start it in a recognized business location. It will also determine whether you work on a part-time basis while maintaining your job, or whether you quit your job to devote full time to the business immediately. Here's how Jeff D., an $8,000-a-year school teacher, evaluated his situation:

House Payment	$ 140
Car Payment	95
Food	120
Clothes	75
Taxes and Insurance	80
Entertainment	40
Incidental Expenses	30
Monthly Outlay	$ 580
	× 12
Annual Outlay	$ 6,860

He decided he needed to keep his job because he had some qualms about turning any sort of profit during his first year. Furthermore, the surplus ($8,000 − 6,860 or $1,140) that he could save out of his salary each year would permit him to expand his business without touching savings he accumulated in the past (except for his starting money). Jeff opened a men's pants store which sold only jeans. He started with $500 of his own money and $4,500 of borrowed money. His wife tended the store weekdays till he got home from school. Jeff was able to quit his job after the store made a $15,000 profit the first year.

Could Jeff have gained by quitting his job before he opened his "Jean Store"? Probably not. By continuing to work, Jeff had a total income of $23,000 that year. His teaching salary paid living expenses. Hence the profits were ploughed back into the business. If Jeff had quit his job, he probably wouldn't have been able to borrow the $4,500 in the first place. Even if he could have borrowed the money and started the business, the monthly withdrawal of $580 for living expenses from the profits probably would have resulted in a cash bind that would have limited his total profit to less than $10,000 a year.

MAKE EVERY CENT COUNT

Many individuals who are starting new businesses are carried away by unnecessary gadgetry. They invest money in fixtures that aren't needed, in service instruments that aren't needed, and often overstock their inventories. Make every cent that you put into your new business venture count by taking advantage of these "insider" cost-saving steps:

1. Get used fixtures
2. Build your own fixtures
3. Get used tools and equipment
4. Buy inventory conservatively

5. Try to avoid slow-moving inventory
6. Use your car for deliveries instead of buying a truck
7. Take cash discounts
8. Avoid luxuries
9. Learn to say "no."

Make every cent count in your operating expenses, too. I'll have more to say about that in a later chapter.

GO WHERE THE ACTION IS

There is an old axiom in the real estate field that says, "There are three important things about a piece of property. They're location, location, location." Use this big-money thinking in locating your business. Locate your business so it's accessible to the people who will buy your product. The location where people will buy your product may not be as good locally as one you might find in another community or another geographical area. *So go where the action is!* Look for a prosperous community with a large and diverse industrial payroll if you're going into a business that depends on individual buying. If you're going into a business that involves specialized buying, go where the specialized buying is done. A wholesale produce house should be located in a market area or in the vicinity of other wholesale produce houses. If you're going into a retailing activity, put yourself in an area that has high traffic and accessible parking. If you're going to wholesale, locate yourself so that you can make deliveries to your customers conveniently.

DON'T PIDDLE WITH TWO-BIT VENTURES

Don't piddle with two-bit ventures. There are many businesses that have notoriously small incomes due to the type of business, the value of the goods sold or the services performed, or low demand for the product or services offered. Avoid these businesses like the plague.

For example, a small shoeshine stand doesn't hold much promise. You may get paid for labor, but it's hard to get profit in addition. You'd have a hard time competing in the manufacture of paper clips or safety pins because they're low-cost, high-volume items. A vending machine route with single machine locations is difficult to service at a profit because there isn't enough volume. Poodle grooming is a lousy business for a small town where there aren't enough poodles. A twelve-unit motel that nets $6,000 a year for the owner — provided the owner does all the work — isn't a worthwhile business because the so-called net is really just a mediocre salary. There's really no profit or return on the investment for the owner.

Chapter 4

MAKE HUNDREDS OF DOLLARS
WITHOUT INVESTING A CENT

YOU DON'T NEED A CENT TO START

I want to emphasize that you don't really need a cent to get started. The possibility was mentioned briefly in Chapter One. Now, in this chapter, we'll learn how and why the possibility exists — *Why you can start a business without a single cent!*

Business schools, where aspiring business leaders pay thousands of dollars for a formal business education, tell their students that every business needs resources. The basic resource is money. With it you can acquire the facilities, tools, materials, and the services of men (labor and management) that make up the classic resources of industry:

Capital
Management
Labor
Facilities (Plants, Machines, Tools)
Material

The truth of the matter is that the required magnitude of each of these resources varies from zero to billions in cash, equipment and materials, and from one person to hundreds of thousands in manpower. Hence, one man or woman — *You* — can provide all the management and labor that is required to start and run a business. And *you don't have to invest a cent because:*

You already have the required facilities and tools — and/or
Someone else has made the cash investment — and/or
Raw materials are available at no cost.

We've made these insider points previously. I emphasize them here because it is important that you have a keen sensitivity to the availability of free, leaseable, hirable, buy-able resources that, if you must buy, you pay for after you've collected your money. This is the way the big-money men operate. I also emphasize these points to separate clearly the important roles you play as:

Manager
Worker

in your own business. These talents are available to you as a result of important resources that have been God-given and developed by you during your lifetime. If you'll harness these resources fully and develop them to a higher degree of capability, the sky is the limit for you, and you don't need a cent to start! Let's call these resources X, Y, and Z. What are they worth?

USE RESOURCE X TO MAKE
$5 TO $50 AN HOUR

Resources X and Y each have bottom values of $5 per hour. They have probable top values of $50 for Resource X and $200 for Resource Y. Resource Z is worth $10 to $1000 or more an hour. By combining these resources and putting Resources X plus Y plus Z to work, it is possible to earn $1000 to $1,000,000 an hour. The people who earn the upper limits (in some cases exceed them) are the leaders. They're the outstanding men who develop these resources to their uppermost limits. Although you may not develop your resources to these high potentials, you certainly can achieve high earning value by developing these resources further.

Resource X can make you earn from $5 to $50 an hour. Resource X is *manual skill.* The product that you can offer as a result of manual skill (either acquired or possible to acquire) includes labor, service, repairs, jobs that no one else will do, and continuous jobs that come under the category of long-term employment. In a society where automation and computers are mechanizing manufacturing, record keeping, mathematics, and routine services, the emphasis in career training and career pursuit is on technology. As a net result, there is a shortage of people with manual skills to keep the products that we manufacture running, to perform services that must be performed by human beings, to take care of the day to day maintenance jobs associated with homes and other properties, to perform jobs that are commonly classified as labor, and to perform jobs for which any given consumer has only an occasional demand. To find a marketable Resource X, look for one or more of these characteristics:

1. Individual consumer demand is occasional (automotive and appliance repairs)

2. Routine service ordinarily performed by home-owner (lawn and garden care)
3. Special skill or training required (plumbing, air conditioning service)
4. Ordinary or distasteful jobs that nobody wants to do (trash removal, janitorial services, cesspool cleaning)
5. A service that is needed but is bothersome (routine maintenance such as filter changing, machine lubrication, etc.)

To realize the top per-hour earnings through the exploitation of your manual skills, sell individual jobs on an individual basis to a large number of different individuals. For example, if you're quoting a person a price for mowing a lawn, quote on the basis of the entire job. Say, "$10 to do the job." Don't say, "I'll do the job for $5 an hour."

RESOURCE Y CAN EARN
$5 TO $200 AN HOUR

Resource Y involves skills over and beyond physical skills and pertains to the use of your *human relations* and *verbal skills*. Resource Y enables you to provide services in people-to-people contacts which involve such things as sales, public relations, customer relations, speaking, lecturing, counseling, recruiting, and similar activities. Most of the big money that is made through the utilization of Resource Y is made in the field of sales. Actually the top limit here is much greater than $200 an hour. However, as a big-ticket salesman, you may work for quite a few hours before you make a sale. Consequently your average pay per hour doesn't equal the commission that you earn during the hour that you make the sale.

In order to develop Resource Y to its optimum, study books in personal development, public relations, public speaking, salesmanship, and psychology. Develop your capability to get along with other people and your capability to speak. Always put your best foot forward with respect to appearance, grooming, posture, and the way you transport yourself. You'll learn more about developing Resource Y in the remainder of this chapter and in Chapters Eight and Thirteen.

RESOURCE Z IS WORTH $10 TO $1000 AN HOUR

Resource Z is your *disciplined* and *creative mind*. Your creative mind is the portion of your mind which develops and generates new ideas, new concepts, and creative works. The disciplined portion of your mind is the part of your mind in which you've implanted knowledge about specific fields or skills, and about the totality of things around you.

Your per-hour earnings through the application of Resource Z will tend to stay at the lower portion of the pay scale if you perform only lower-level creative works, such as making clever novelties. Your per-hour earnings tend to rise to the high end of the pay scale when you perform higher order creative works. These involve such things as invention and the development of new business concepts.

X PLUS Y PLUS Z CAN EARN $50 to $1,000,000 AN HOUR

When you combine X, Y, and Z, you come up with a powerful combination of resources that have a fantastic earning capability. Any activity or process in which the sum of several parts is greater than their sums taken individually is a "synergistic" situation. This is the kind of situation that prevails when you combine Resources X, Y, and Z. Here are some typical situations in which individuals have used Resources X, Y, and Z in synergistic combination.

An air conditioning repairman was called in to service an air conditioner. He found that the compressor in the air conditioner was bad and that a replacement would cost $200.

If he had been an employee of an air conditioning company, he would have been paid by the hour for his work. In this case he's operating principally with Resource X. If he's in business for himself, he might go on to sell a better compressor and hence realize a larger profit. Thus he also puts more Resource Y to work. However, he might sell a new and larger air conditioning system to his customer by suggesting the addition of cooling to an unused room. Consequently, he's utilizing some Resource Z and he has opened the avenue for still higher dollar-per-hour earnings.

A rental agent shows a prospective tenant a property. In spite of his capable use of Resource Y in doing a selling job, he cannot convince the prospective tenant that he has the kind of space he wants. Then, using Resource Z, he evolves a concept for remodeling one of the spaces to exactly fit the needs of the tenant. The premium rent that he can collect for meeting the prospective tenant's needs will pay for the alterations that have to be made and for the rental fee as well. He's increased his earning power by applying Resource Z.

OPPORTUNITIES THAT YOU CAN HARNESS WITH RESOURCE X

There are a large number of moneymaking activities that employ Resource X. Here are just a few of them, with some ideas for getting started:

> Property repairs and maintenance (Start with tools you have now)
>
> Janitorial service (Joe B's. success, Chapter Two, will give you some ideas)
>
> Dressmaking (Why not specialize in wedding dresses and formals?)
>
> Lawn and garden maintenance (Canvass neighborhoods with medium- to high-cost houses)
>
> Plumbing repairs (Give "free plumbing inspection" to get started)

Animal grooming (Check city and county license records to find dog owners)

Laundry service (Give "in at 9, out at 5" service)

Handicraft manufacture (Quilts, shawls, pillows, decoupage, etc.)

Automobile body work (Go to customer's house to do minor jobs)

Motor repairs (Build an inventory and give exchange service)

Carpentry (Build cabinets)

Photography (Specialize in wedding and family pictures)

Insect exterminating (Give free inspections)

Duplicating service (Give one-day service. Solicit social and fraternal organizations)

Delivery service (Start with your car)

Fire extinguisher service (Make free inspections)

Dirt moving and excavation (Solicit building contractors)

Painting (Give one-day service)

Boat making (Start in your garage)

Trailer manufacture (Make specials built-to-order)

Key making (Go to customer's house with portable equipment; (solicit property owners for "duplicate" business)

Sign painting (Start by getting placard jobs from supermarkets and department stores)

Hairdressing (Start in your home if local zoning ordinances permit it)

Rug cleaning (Pursue apartment and office businesses; check tax rolls to identify building owners)

Although the activities listed require some Y and Z skill in addition to X skill, these activities are predominantly X activities. Some involve jobs which others aren't anxious to perform; most involve services that are difficult to find when you need them. This list is by no means all-inclusive, and I am sure that as you ponder the list you'll think of numerous other activities which involve Resource X that you are qualified to offer.

WAYS TO CAPITALIZE ON RESOURCE Y

Here are just a few of the many ways in which you can capitalize on Resource Y, your ability to deal with people and to express yourself verbally, with some thoughts on getting started:

Retail sales (Sell direct door-to-door or take a commission sales job)

Wholesale sales (Sell janitorial supplies, paper goods, etc., direct to businesses, or sell jewelry, hardware, etc., to dealers for re-sale)

Customer relations (Call on newcomers to town and tell them about businesses which retain you)

Public relations (Write publicity releases, promote fund-raising activities, etc.)

Speech coaching (Solicit banks, industry, etc., for executive students)

Ticket agency (Offer special "package" deals)

Entertaining (Advertise in classified "personals" to entertain at parties)

Radio-TV announcing (Moonlight on a local station)

Teaching (Moonlight in a college, trade or business school)

Real estate sales (Learn the ropes as a salesman from a broker)

Sales recruiting (Get into a pyramid selling situation; you "pyramid" the sales organization by recruiting other salesmen, and you get a percentage of the sales of your recruits)

Personnel recruiting (Use connections in industries that you're familiar with)

Property leasing (Specialize in specific types of property; e.g., offices)

Manufacturer's representative (See Thomas Directory to find manufacturers to represent)

Telephone answering service (Solicit doctors, manufacturer's reps, salesmen, and businesses)

Stock broker (Take a job with one of the giants who'll train you)

Employment agency (You need a license in most states for this one)

Insurance sales (Take the job that offers the most training)

These activities may involve some use of Resource X or Resource Z, but they're activities in which Resource Y is the dominant and highly important one. This list should serve to provide numerous other ideas for ways in which to capitalize on your Resource Y.

HOW TO CASH IN ON RESOURCE Z

It's an easy matter to make a list of the disciplined knowledge areas which employ Resource Z. The mental creative aspect of Resource Z is sometimes a little more difficult to pinpoint. Here's a list of areas and activities in which Resource Z is the dominant factor:

Invention (Start by trying to determine what's needed)

Business formation (Develop a business idea fully and form a corporation; Chapter Six tells how to do it)

Accounting (Go to the client's place of business or home to do the work)

Interior decorating (Line up with furniture stores)

Research and development (Stick to the field of research you know best)

Electronics design and services (Service industrial electronic controls)

Air conditioning design and services (Give free inspection)

Creative writing (Study the magazine or publisher you're
 going to write for and slant your material to fit)
Speech writing (Solicit bank and industry PR depart-
 ments)
Furniture design (Submit designs to manufacturers on a
 speculative basis)
Advertising (Take a job in an agency to learn the ropes)
Machine design (Offer services to machine manufacturers
 and factory owners)
Creative art (Make arrangements with galleries or de-
 partment stores for outlet)
Architecture (Take a job with an established firm)
Sales strategy (Offer this service to retailers)
Investment counseling (This is a good side line for a full-
 time investor)
Law
Engineering
Music
Dentistry
Medicine
Management

The X, Y, and Z categories refer to kinds of resources
rather than level of achievement and endeavor. Nevertheless,
the highest achievements and endeavors are those that result
through the use of Resource Z. Resource Y ranks next, and
Resource X tends to be at the lowest level. This does not
necessarily mean that Resource X will always earn less than
Resource Z, nor does it mean that a considerable amount of
formal training is essential to the development of Resource
Z. Anyone can develop any or all of these skills to whatever level he wishes to develop them, within God-given
limits. But God has been generous! Few of us utilize even
10 per cent of the power God has endowed us with.

HOW TO DEVELOP RESOURCE X

If you're strong on manual skill, you can enter a business which offers manual skills with a high assurance of success. As your business grows, you can develop your Y and Z resources and hire others to do the Resource X work. But at the outset, you will be more successful and build your business faster by developing your own Resource X to its fullest and getting maximum results from it.

A pure, manual "Resource X" concept is not realistic. There's always some Resource Z coupled to it, and there's sometimes some Resource Y involved. The development of your manual skills to the point of highest employment involves knowing the most and being the best in your field of endeavor. To do this, learn the manual skills that you perform best through study, observation, and practice. For example, Barry Stanton had some ability to repair small machines; he refined his skill by studying manufacturer's manuals and catalogs, and took advantage of special training to learn typewriter repair. He worked out ways to do his work faster and better to increase his hourly yield. As his business grew, he worked out ways to segregate his work so that routine jobs requiring less manual skill could be performed by less valuable helpers. Thus he began to build his managerial know-how so that he was able to run the larger organization that his business grew into more efficiently and profitably.

HOW TO DEVELOP YOUR RESOURCE Y

Whether the actual saleable output of your business is Resource X, Y, or Z, you'll make more money at it if you have a well-developed Resource Y. Resource Y makes sales, and sales feed a business. Feed a business plenty of sales and it soon grows into a husky star with even a marginal exercise of good management. Starve a business of sales and it soon dies, as a failure, no matter how well the rest of it is run. Resource Y, human relations and verbal abilities, puts a business across by inspiring sales, getting maximum results from employees, and by winning financial support (for expansion or in bad times) when a business needs it.

To develop your human relations skills, study books on personal development,* psychology, salesmanship and human relations. Observe people that you like, and learn why you like them. Try to win friends through sincere gestures. Don't play-act or flatter; give sincere compliments and avoid stinging criticism. Put your best foot forward by dressing neatly and staying well groomed. That's the way winners operate.

To develop your verbal skills, practice talking to yourself with a tape recorder. Listen, then repeat and try to improve. Join the Toastmaster's Organization; it will help you become a better speaker and a better conversationalist.

A DAILY PLAN FOR SHARPENING RESOURCE Z

You can develop and sharpen Resource Z without engaging in a long, formal education program. Formal education provides tremendous benefits. However, if you are unable to pursue formal education as a result of your social, economic, or chronological situation, this doesn't mean that you must continue to use Resource Z in its present state of development. As a matter of fact, most people are held back because they stopped learning when they reached the age of 12, 21, or 25. By engaging in an easy daily program for sharpening Resources Z you can improve its power 5, 10, even 100 times. Here's why.

Your mind generates ideas that can be converted into cash. The automotive, air conditioning, TV and other in-

---

The Miracle Success System — A Scientific Way To Get What You Want In Life, by Forrest H. Frantz, Sr., Parker Publishing Company, provides a comprehensive program for developing Resources Y and Z.

dustries started as ideas. Your mind enables you to provide solutions to problems in the business world as well as in the other facets of your life. Your mind enables you to arrive at decisions that can change the course of your life, such as what kind of business to start. It stores and retains memories that are profitable or can be made profitable, such as a promotion gimmick in another field that you can employ in your business. Furthermore, your mind enables you to learn new specialized skills, and it can influence. Your mind's influence can spread to other people, but even more importantly: *Your mind influences your outlook and what you do in your business and in your life.* Your day is as good as the mental attitude you develop when you awake in the morning. Here are five things which you can do each day to develop the power of your mind:

1. Concentrate on finding, planning, and developing your own business;
2. Search for ideas to make it possible;
3. Study a new skill for one hour each day till you've mastered it;
4. Look about you for problems that require creative solutions, and as a practice exercise, try to solve them;
5. Make firm decisions to get things done and follow through in implementing these decisions.

There's no point in merely exercising your mind for the fun of it. While you're developing it, you might as well achieve some concrete results. So concentrate on finding, planning and developing your own business. The previous chapters and the chapters which follow should trigger off a number of ideas and ways for implementing them. This book should help you to pinpoint specific businesses that you can enter with the resources that you have available — both personally, financially, and in terms of other material resources.

START A NOTEBOOK

I suggest that you start a notebook. Label it, "Business Venture Planning." Jot down every idea that comes to mind concerning the potential businesses that you might enter in this book. Use this book to collect notes from your reading, your studies, and your conversations with other people. Hence you'll be concentrating on a real goal, and all of the effort that you expend will be productive in turning you down the path to riches.

Your concentration on developing your own business will lead you to search for ideas that will make it possible. You'll encounter impediments and possible problems. However, if you permit this concentration to motivate you to search for ideas and means, you'll find ideas coming from sources that you never dreamed of. Some possible places to find ideas are your public library, businesses, your friends and associates, magazines and books, and government publications. Whenever you get or hear an idea that you think might be of some use to you, jot it down and stick it in your pocket. Transfer these idea notes to your "Business Venture Planning" notebook each evening. Before you know it, you'll have all kinds of ideas that will fit together and help you achieve your goal.

Study some new skill or area of activity for one hour each day in order to expand the base of knowledge from which you can work. By studying one hour each day, you can learn quite a bit about accounting in twenty days. You'll hardly be an expert, but you will be considerably better versed in this field. It would be productive for you to do the same thing with a number of other business skills. The broader the base of knowledge that you have to work from, the greater your chances of success in any activity that you undertake.

One of the most important factors in achieving success in any endeavor is the ability to identify and pinpoint problems that exist. Once you know the problem is there, you need to understand the problem. After you understand the problem, what's known, what's unknown, what's good and what's bad, you can pursue the systematic solution of the problem. So look about you each day for problems, for areas where improvements can be made, and for more efficient ways to do things. Look at the various facets of the problem, see if you can rearrange them, if you can change an element of the problem, or if you can reach solutions by combining things.

MAKE FIRM DECISIONS

Make firm decisions and follow through on them. Don't spend a lot of time making a decision and then worrying about it afterward. The time to get through with the worry is before you make the decision. Once you have made it, follow through on the decision with the firm conviction that the result will be exactly as you planned it. A decision for a solution that is not always the best will still turn out to be an effective one if you follow through and do the job as you planned it. Review the decisions that you make each day, and the way in which you are implementing them and the ones that you have made on previous days.

If you'll follow this simple five-point plan daily, you'll realize continually improving results and potential utilization of your Resource Z.

Chapter 5

A FOOLPROOF STRATEGY FOR SELECTING YOUR QUICK-PROFIT BUSINESS

CHOOSE THE RIGHT BUSINESS AND REAP A BUNDLE

Choose the right business to enter and you're off to a good start. Then work the resources properly and you'll make money. The choice of business isn't a magic "pick the one and only — or you'll fail" deal. There are probably several hundred different businesses that you might enter with reasonable chances of success. However, you can probably narrow the field down to five to ten best and optimum possibilities for you.

In the preceding chapters, we've introduced a number of business possibilities requiring various amounts of starting capital, a wide array of disciplines, and touching on each of the ten fundamental business areas. In this chapter you'll be introduced to a Selection Matrix, which will enable you to make a more optimum choice of businesses to enter. Then you'll be introduced to a number of strategies and rules of business conduct that have turned paupers into millionaires and made the sophisticated businessman and insider even richer.

THE TEN QUESTION BUSINESS SELECTION TEST

There's a broad array of criteria to consider in picking the business in which you'll launch your ascent to profit. The factors that you'll want to consider include:

1. What do I like to do?
2. What skills do I possess?
3. What potential do my hobby interests have?
4. How much capital do I have?
5. How much additional capital can I raise?
6. Will my business be full- or part-time?
7. Will I have a regular business location or operate from home?
8. How much do I want to make?
9. Which of the ten opportunity fields do I want to tap?
10. What business is most needed in the proposed locality?

Take this ten question test. Then you'll be ready to use the Selection Matrix and the balance of this chapter to better advantage. Here's how the test works:

Leslie S., age twenty-nine, works in a furniture factory putting the upholstery on furniture. His hobbies are hunting and fishing. He has saved $1,200 and he has a net worth of about $7,000. He presently earns $900 a month. He is married and has two children, ages three and seven. He has a high school education and keeps his home in repair himself. He's handy at plumbing, electrical and carpentry repairs.

Running through the ten question test, the answers (keyed to the questions above) come out like this:

1. Skilled hand work
2. Upholstery, carpentry, and general handy-man skills
3. Hunting lodge operation, game warden, sporting goods sales
4. $1,200 plus about $300 in tools
5. Probably 1/3 of net worth — a little over $2,000
6. Part time would be safe and guarantee a mimimum income of more than $900
7. If I go part time, I ought to work it from my home
8. I'd like to clear $300 a month the first year, $600 a month the second year, and then go full time, earning $2,000 a month
9. An upholstery shop (service) looks like the best bet
10. Les found there were no upholstery shops in his town (population of 25,000 people), a more than adequate market for an upholstery business.

On the basis of these answers, Leslie S. probably will begin an upholstery shop in his garage. He'll probably solicit furniture stores, apartment house owners and managers, and large industries with considerable office facilities for business. In addition, he might solicit the business of individuals through classified ads. Note that he has more than enough capital for a service business and can even take advantage of quantity buying for commonly used materials and supplies.

Alternate avenues open to Leslie would be direct sales of sporting goods, the purchase of a wooded tract of land for week-end development into a hunting lodge, or a fix-it business.

THE SELECTION MATRIX

A matrix is an array of symbols arranged horizontally and vertically. Make yourself a copy of the selection matrix,

Table 1, on a large sheet of paper without the question marks and X's shown. On your own copy of the selection matrix, put a question mark in each spot where the activity is specialized or limited for you. Put an X in each spot where you feel you have adequate or unlimited capability, in the manner shown on the sample. Then simply draw a horizontal line across the matrix through each of the ten areas in which you have some skill or experience.

Table 1   Selection Matrix

X — Adequate; ? — Perhaps; Blank — Doubtful

	$10	$100	$1,000	$10,000
Creative/Technical	x	x	x	x
Service	x	x	x	x
Construction			?	x
Manufacturing	?	?	?	x
Selling	x	?	x	x
Trading	x	x	x	x
Finance & Investment			?	x
Rentals		?	x	x
Natural Resources	?	?	x	x
People Resources	?	x	x	x

Draw a vertical line through the approximate amounts of money that you have available. This will prove helpful in finding an area that matches your pocketbook and skills. Where these lines cross on a question mark or an "X," you have a business possibility.

After you've completed the matrix, review your answers to the Ten Question Business Selection Test. Then review the lists of specific possibilities cited in earlier chapters. Underline each of the specific possibilities that fit you, and enter the possibility in your "Business Venture Planning" note-book. Then study the balance of this chapter with these possibilities in mind. Chances are that by the time you've reached the end of this chapter you'll have narrowed your list down considerably.

HOW TO GET THE DEAL THAT FITS YOU BEST

To get the deal that fits you best, get into an activity that you will enjoy and find exciting. If you pick an activity that is dull and uninteresting to you, you'll soon become dis-enchanted with it and care very little about pursuing it. There is no reason why you shouldn't have fun while you're earning money and building your wealth. If you have a special skill or specialized experience, consider an activity where you can put it to work. If you are skilled in electronics, for example, you might go into electronics servicing, the sale of electronic equipment, manufacture of electronic equipment, or development of new electronic devices. Some people gain specialized experience through schooling, jobs, or hobbies.

PICK BIG-PROFIT VENTURES

Pick big-profit ventures. There's no point in picking a business that involves small profits for large expenditures of effort. Forget about part-time, low-paying jobs as a way to get started unless you're taking the jobs to acquire addition-al experience as well as cash, don't count on them as the way to build big profits. Big profits result from high volume sales with reasonable profit margins or from low-volume, high-dollar sales with reasonable profit margins. If you enter a service venture, your percentage profits are greater be-cause you'll be selling your own time at the outset; con-sequently, you'll be developing profits and you'll be getting paid for your time as well. As your service venture grows, you'll be selling the services of others and paying for them just as you would buy a product to put on a retail shelf. The big difference is that an employee's meter keeps running, and his time costs you whether you sell it or not!

FIND A REPEATER

Find a "repeating" business — one in which you sell the same customers over and over again. By performing a satisfactory service, by manufacturing or by selling a satisfactory product, and by giving your customers satisfaction, you're assured of continuing business. Each time you add a new customer, you simply improve the repeating action.

The classic example of a "repeater" in the manufacturing business is the razor blade. Gillette started it and over the years other manufacturers have followed the pattern. They practically give the razor away in order to sell the blades that fit it. There are many analogies to the razor and the razor blade. For example: phonograph and phonograph records; camera and film; mechanical pencil and leads; ball point pen and refill cartridges.

GET A HIGH PERCENTAGE RETURN ON INVESTMENT CASH

The percentage return on investment is annual dollar return divided by actual cash dollars invested times 100 per cent. Hence, the higher the annual cash return and the lower the initial dollar investment, the greater your return on investment. In selecting a venture, choose one which yields a high return on investment cash. Look for deals that return 20 per cent or better annually, and that possess a minimum of speculation.

PICK A BUSINESS THAT
ATTRACTS CAPITAL

There are certain kinds of businesses that attract investors for one or more reasons. Some of the reasons why investors prefer one investment to another are:

1. High return on investment
2. Tax advantages
3. Minimized risk
4. Security
5. High technology
6. Glamour

Minimized risk and security were prime objectives in the '30's and were highlighted again early in the '70's when failure of several large corporations resulted in reorganization and bankruptcies. The speculative investor tends to be a venturer and generally isn't as jumpy about security as the conservative investor. He knows he's taking some risk when he enters a speculative venture.

What does this mean to you? If you have a nervous disposition and tend to worry, stay away from high speculation, high risk ventures. Seek the less risky, surer return businesses and investments, even if return is lower and slower.

MINIMIZE YOUR RISK

You can minimize your risk in starting your business. Moonlighting is one way to do it. The moonlighter retains his steady job, which provides food, shelter, and the other necessities of life for his family. This is the route Leslie S. took. Consequently, he won't have to count on his venture as a means of livelihood. If he encounters difficulty in getting it started, he hasn't risked everything, and he can take time to get things running smoothly.

Here are some other ways to minimize risks in your business venture:

1. Hedge
2. Cover all transactions in writing
3. Sell services for cash
4. Carry insurance
5. Incorporate
6. Share risk with other investors
7. Diversify

You can hedge by making counter-balancing investments so that if one loses, another gains. For example, if you go into appliance sales, a repair service department will provide income when hard times cause new appliance sales to go down. Bolster a seasonal business (such as air conditioning service) with an off-season item; e.g., air conditioning and heating, lawnmowers and snow plows, etc.

Cover all transactions in writing to avoid later misunderstanding or *slanted interpretation.* It's easy for human error or intentional twisting to create problems on verbal deals. When it's in writing, it's clear to all parties; if it comes to a legal test, the written document prevails.

Why sell for cash only? Because it eliminates a lot of headaches, reduces risk, and reduces your operating cash requirements. Later, when you're established, you can extend credit to increase your business. Then, extend credit only to good credit risks who can pass thorough credit checking.

Minimize risk with fire, theft, and liability insurance. If you manufacture a product or sell foods, carry product liability insurance.

You minimize risk by incorporating because your liability is limited to the capitalization of your corporation. You can reduce the consequences of a business failure by diluting your equity and sharing the risks of business with other investors.

Diversification is the expansion of your business into several product areas. Hence, if you manufacture defense products, you can diversify into consumer products to minimize the impact of reduced defense budgets. If you manufacture a product or provide a service that sells only in the summer, you can diversify into a winter sales or service item to make year-round use of your capabilities.

It isn't smart money if you take risky chances with it!

KEEP IT EASY TO MANAGE

Pick a business that is easy to manage and keep it that way. A business can be effective only when it is managed properly. Choose a business that is easy to manage so that you can keep things under control and enjoy life more. If you keep the management of your business simple, you also have greater freedom when you prosper enough to turn the management over to someone else. For example, a small dry-cleaning business is hard to manage because it requires selling, pick-up and delivery, store-front sales, and a cleaning-pressing plant operation. It's a lot to manage and operate with small volume.

HOW TO GET IN FOR THE LOWEST DOLLAR COST

Only an idiot would attempt to start a business by investing all of his resources or only his own resources. *The astute businessman attempts to invest as little of his own money as possible.* He acquires additional money by borrowing or selling part ownership (an equity interest) in his existing business or in the new investment. He pledges assets that he may have or potentials that have asset value as collateral or security for loans. The only sound business proposition is one that will bring in enough income to service his debt as payments fall due and also provide adequate profits to pay the interest.

Using other people's money is only part of the strategy of getting into a business for the lowest cost. The absolute criteria for lowest dollar investment revolves around the price that you pay to enter an endeavor. You can generally buy any advertised business for less than the quoted price. You may have to do a lot of negotiating and you may have to wait a while in order to make your deal. If the time and delays involved in negotiating will not penalize you, it's smart to take your time. Negotiate for the lowest price before you make a deal.

If you're buying a business, look it over thoroughly before you make an offer. Observe the traffic in and out of the store. Try to make an estimate of the store's sales, and make a note of the business activities in the neighborhood. Then crosscheck against other businesses of the same type in the locality where you'll be doing businesses, as well as with similar businesses in other localities.

Signs of lowest cost opportunities include businesses that are in trouble, properties that are unsightly or are run-down, distress merchandise, and other bargain situations. Some people make a living looking for "bargains." But beware! A bargain that doesn't offer a profit opportunity is not a bargain.

SECURITY/PROFIT TRADE-OFFS

A high security investment generally does not yield as much income as a "speculative" investment. First mortgages and insured savings are tops for security, but the yield is low. High-rated bonds are, in effect, first mortgages. However, a spate of corporate liquidity problems in 1970 cast a shadow of doubt on this when some bonds dropped to a low percentage of their face value — in at least one case to 15 per cent! The basic point is that property values can drop, and when the property is a business, the value drops when the business performs poorly. Hence nothing is sacred, and security is a matter of degree.

If you're going to make a shoestring start and want growth you'll have to make security secondary, but that doesn't mean you ought to ignore it. Here are some methods for maintaining maximum relative security while building your own venture:

1. If you have a job, keep it and moonlight your business to a successful start.
2. If you form a partnership, all but one of the partners should have and keep their jobs.
3. If your wife can work for an established firm while you start your own business, you have a security plus.
4. Plan your business as thoroughly as possible before you commit dollars.
5. Avoid long-term commitments such as leases and employment contracts if you can do so without risking loss of a good location or skilled employees.
6. Keep investments in capital equipment and inventory at the lowest possible level consistent with efficient operation.

LAST, BUT FOREMOST

Last on our Ten Question Business Selection Test was: "What business is most needed in the proposed locality?"

This question is of foremost importance in deciding on a business. To operate a successful business, you need sales. To make sales, there must be a "need." Without a need, you can't sell. The locality which you're considering probably has needs for a number of different kinds of businesses. If you can provide the most needed, highest volume, highest profit business, you'll make the optimum kill. Provided, of course, it fits your capital, desires, and a host of other criteria highlighted by the Selection Matrix and the Ten Question Business Selection Test.

You need sales. Your best chance of getting them exists

if there's a need, there's no competition, you've got the best location in town, and you build an outstanding reputation quickly. On the other hand, it would be foolish to start a drugstore in a town of 5,000 with four drugstores, two of which are going broke. Lots of people make this mistake and fail in business. Don't let it happen to you. There has to be a market, and your share of it has to be adequate to support your business.

YOUR THREE MAJOR OBJECTIVES

You can make money if you make up your mind to do it and put a determined effort into accomplishment. Every successful business in the United States bears testimony to this. The largest department store in town is the descendant of a very small store. Keep your mind on three major objectives in everything you do.

First, operate at a profit. The dollars that pass through your hands don't enrich you. The dollars you take in and keep are your profits. The size of your profits determines your ability to reach the next objective.

The second objective is growth. You want your business to grow from week to week, month to month, and year to year. You make it grow by increasing your customer or client following, by increasing the scope of goods or services that you offer, and by re-investing profits wisely.

The third objective is leadership. You achieve leadership by providing quality products and outstanding service. Keep these objectives in mind as you plan each step of your venture.

Chapter 6

HOW TO GET STARTING
CAPITAL EASILY

Dennis R. wanted to start his own business. He was a garage mechanic, and he was pretty good at automatic transmissions. He decided to open a transmission shop. His needs stacked up something like this:

Equipment	$ 5,000
Inventory	$ 1,000
Advance Rent	$ 1,500
Opening Advertising	$ 1,000
Operating Reserve	$ 1,500
	$10,000

He had only $100 that he felt he could venture in the

business. However, when we reviewed his situation, we found these pertinent facts:

1. Cash in savings $ 500
2. U.S. Savings Bonds   400
3. Equity in home   2,000
4. Equipment suitable for his business   500
5. Old furniture in basement worth   150
6. Automobile (Clear) $1,500

Here's how it worked out:

Cash Start		$ 100
Step 1: Sold old furniture		150
	Cash Now	$ 250
Step 2: Cashed in savings bonds		400
	Cash Now	$ 650
Step 3: Borrowed on Signature		$1,000
	Cash Now	$1,650
Step 4: 2nd lien on house		1,500
	Cash Now	$3,150
Step 5: Refinance automobile		1,000
	Cash Now	$4,150
Step 6: Since he already owned $500 worth of equipment, he needed only $4,500 worth of "new" equipment. By shopping around, he found used equipment to fill his needs for $1,500 cash.		1,500
	Cash Now	$3,650
Step 7: He refinanced the equipment for		2,000
	Cash Now	$5,650

This exceeded his requirement by $650.

This is not an unusual example. He reduced his starting

costs by being resourceful, and he borrowed on resources that he had available. Note that his savings were left intact. He set up a debt service requirement for the future which could be handled out of earnings.

The purpose of this chapter is to show you how to use a relatively small nest egg, just as Dennis R. did, to raise large amounts of money for your business ventures and business activities.

HOW TO GET LOTS OF MONEY WITH A SMALL NEST EGG

Most large fortunes are built through the use of other people's money in augmentation to the entrepreneur's own available capital. You can borrow considerable amounts of money with a relatively small nest egg. The amount of money that you can borrow is a function of your net worth, your proven past performance, your knowledge of finance and business, and your ability as a salesman. In many instances, a good idea may put you into a position to obtain 100 per cent financing. It's sometimes possible to obtain 110 per cent and even 120 per cent financing. Although this may sound fantastic, it's done frequently in the real estate world.

The technique of using a large amount of borrowed money and investing a minimum amount of your own capital is "leverage." It follows that if you can get a 10 per cent return on invested dollars, the more dollars you invest, the greater your profit dollars are going to be. Consequently, if you can earn 10 per cent on $100,000, you will earn $10,000, while 10 per cent on $1,000 is only $100. Even if it costs you 8 per cent for borrowed money to realize the 10 per cent profit, you still have a net profit of 2 per cent on borrowed money and 10 per cent on your own. The rewards increase as the profit percentage goes up and the interest cost goes down. If you can earn 20 per cent on your investment with 6 per cent money, you have a net gain of 14 per cent. Hence, a 14 per cent net return on $1,000 of borrowed money would be $140, while a 14 per cent net return on $100,000 of borrowed money would be $14,000.

It isn't difficult to obtain large amounts of money when you have a small nest egg. A lender generally wants collateral. Here are some of the things that you can use as collateral:

Land and buildings
Stocks
Bonds
Certificates of Deposit
Equipment (Automotive, factory, etc.)
Leases
Furniture and jewelry
Insurance policies
Bonded warehouse receipts
Business equities
Accounts receivable

You may have additional assets that you're prone to overlook which enhance your net worth position. These include:

Savings accounts
Credit union savings
Company investment programs
Pension plans
Antiques
Valuable collections

It isn't always essential that you have collateral. You can sometimes obtain signature loans on the basis of your reputation, or you may be able to obtain a signature loan by providing a compensating balance. Compensating balances can be rented. This drives up the cost of getting money. We'll have more to say about this in succeeding sections.

THE BASIC METHODS FOR FINANCING YOUR SUCCESSFUL BUSINESS

There are several methods for financing your business. They are:

1. Proprietorship, in which you invest your own cash and/or borrowed money;
2. A partnership, which increases resources but dilutes your personal equity;
3. A corporation, which increases resources but dilutes your personal equity.

WHERE TO BORROW MONEY AND GET CREDIT

In following any of the routes based on debt financing, you can utilize any of the collateral and loan-getting techniques that have been and will be discussed. Here are some of the sources to tap for loans:

Banks (Signature loans, loans collateralized with leases, equipment, autos, real estate, etc.)

Savings and loan institutions (Mortgage loans secured by real estate)

Government agencies (Government direct loans as through SBA, or government-guaranteed loans. SBA, FHA, and other agencies guarantee loans.)

Insurance companies (Mortgage loans)

Finance companies (Short-term loans secured by equipment)

Relatives

Friends

In addition to using collateral and some of the other loan-getting and securing techniques cited, there are a number of other methods that can be used to obtain loans. For example, Bill S. buys equipment, such as a bench saw for his woodwork shop, on a thirty to ninety day open account. This is, in effect, a non-interest-bearing loan secured by the equipment that he purchased. Another method is to use reciprocity, as Chuck does by giving some of his business to somebody in return for a loan. He's given an insurance agent friend some of his insurance business for a loan.

In effect, all of your open accounts provide you with borrowing power. The cost of the equipment or merchandise that is charged puts capital into your business. Another technique for securing a loan without calling it just that is to get paid partially or in full in advance for services begun now or to be rendered at some future date, as I do in some of my consulting transactions. If you build to a special order, e.g., a customer trailer, get a substantial advance payment. One typical method by which advance payment is secured for services is the monthly or annual retainer method, and another is the service policy method.

THE PROS AND CONS OF DEBT AND EQUITY FINANCING

Regardless of the form of organization that you choose, there'll usually be some debt financing involved. If you maintain a sole proprietorship, all of your financing will be debt financing. If you take in a partner, you'll initially finance your business through "equity" dilution; that is, you give up some of the business and consequently some of the profits in order to put additional capital into the business. For example, Foster M. formed a corporation to manufacture golf carts and sold stock to others. He ended up with 20 per cent ownership, but he raised the cash needed to enter a business that he couldn't have afforded to enter with his own limited resources. His "equity" in the business decreased; the capital in the business increased.

The sole proprietorship is often resource-limited. It is limited to your capital and to your borrowing power. The advantages of the sole proprietorship are that you are your own boss, you save a lot of lost time and motion discussing and getting concurrence from others, and you reap the full benefits from every effort that you expend. However, the sole proprietorship may penalize you in terms of the limited capital and borrowing power that you can apply. It may also penalize you since you limit the mental and physical resources that go into the business to your own. For example, if you're a good salesman, you might benefit by having an associate with an accounting or management background.

Sometimes partnerships go sour. You may disagree, or your partner may get lazy or turn to bad habits. In a sole proprietorship you have only yourself to reckon with. One proprietor is better off than a pair of mismatched and poorly coordinated partners. A proprietorship, and for that matter a partnership, enjoys tax advantages while income in the business is low. When income reaches a relatively high level (that varies with the specific situation and the year's income tax schedules), the proprietorship and the partnership are penalized.

There are definite advantages to incorporation. The corporation is recognized as a single individual, although many persons may hold stock in it. Hence, liability of the individual stockholders is limited. Hence, if you invest $10,000 in stock, that's all you can lose. It is taxed on a different basis than a proprietorship or a partnership. It is relatively costly to organize and has franchise and sometimes other taxes imposed on it that are not imposed on a proprietorship or a partnership. However, when income becomes large, the corporation has a tax advantage over the individual.

I prefer sole proprietorship with debt financing for most of my activities. This permits me to exercise maximum control, saves a considerable amount of time for me in my operations, and allows me to receive maximum benefits from my efforts. I enter equity business arangements when they afford additional business opportunities that I cannot take advantage of alone. Typical equity situations that appeal to me involve deals that are too big for me to handle singly due to the financial considerations, and business situations that make talents available which I could not otherwise obtain.

MAKE YOUR BANKER WANT TO
LEND YOU MORE MONEY

Bankers and the loan officers of lending institutions want to lend you money. It's an important part of their business and one of the principal means by which they earn profits. But when a loan officer grants a loan, he wants to be sure that it will be repaid under the terms specified. The first thing that he looks for is net worth. If your net worth is large, you can borrow 10 per cent to 20 per cent of your net worth on your signature. He also looks at income. If you are holding a job and starting your business on a moonlight basis, it enhances your ability to repay and consequently to get a loan. Similarly, if your business operation is successful and provides a substantial income, you have an additional plus for obtaining a loan. The first requisite is to place a financial statement in his hands so he can assess your net worth and income. Your bank has standard forms available for personal or corporate financial statements. Here's an example of the net worth portion of the financial statement that a new business venturer took to his banker:

Statement of Net Worth
of Joe Doaks on January 1, 1972

Assets

Continental National Bank (Savings)	$ 1,284
Mercury Savings and Loan (Savings)	3,678
Continental National Bank (Checking)	1,065
Stocks and Bonds	2,050
Home at 1984 Vista Drive	27,500
Rental House at 2937 Bonneville	16,500

Car #1 (two year old Pontiac)	1,400	
(Car #2 (four year old Ford)	500	
Furniture	2,000	
		$55,977
Liabilities		
Mortgage on home	21,600	
Mortgage on rental house	9,300	
		$30,900
Net Worth		$25,077

A loan officer will question you about the purpose of the loan. He'll be more willing to make a loan for investment purposes than for pleasure purposes. If you present him with a neatly documented plan for the way in which you'll apply the loan proceeds, he'll respect your astuteness as a business-man and will more likely grant the loan.

A loan officer looks for collateral, and he is swayed by compensating balances. If you can provide solid collateral, you can almost always obtain a loan without delay or extended conversation. When you can't collateralize the loan, the loan officer can only go on the personal factors that we've just mentioned. However, he looks at an additional factor. He'll check on the checking account balances that you've maintained in the bank. If they're not high enough, he'll ask you to maintain a compensating balance. (A compensating balance frequently takes the form of a savings account deposit.) However, if you maintain adequate balances in your checking account or accounts, this may suffice.

Don't see a loan officer with a wishy-washy attitude. Be convinced that you're going to get the loan before you see him, and prepare your presentation in an orderly fashion so that you can sell him on the loan just as you would sell a product or a service. Remember, the loan officer wants to lend money to you. Make his job easy by selling him on it.

PREPARE A GROWTH PROGRESS REPORT

Your past earnings and business history is an important indication of your capability. It shows the progress that you have made in improving your earning ability. Although this information may not carry the weight that a financial statement carries with a loan officer, it is an important one — it is of interest to him. Simply show your earnings for the last five or ten years. Be prepared to explain why and how you were able to increase your earnings during the years. In the event that your earnings have stayed flat or have gone down, there's no point in doing this.

COMPENSATING BALANCES

The short-term objective of any business is profit. Banks are businesses, and they seek profits. If money costs a bank 7 per cent and it lends to you at 8 per cent, it makes a 1 per cent gross profit. Bank overhead is high, and that cuts the net thin. However, money left in checking accounts doesn't cost the bank anything directly. This gives rise to the mechanism of the "balance" that enables you to borrow money even when the competition for loans is high.

Suppose you want to borrow $5,000. You don't have collateral. You approach your banker for a signature loan. Since you'll probably maintain a minimum balance of $1,000 in your checking account, you indicate this to him. He'll be more likely to make the loan, since the bank really has only $4,000 out while it's collecting interest on $5,000. Bankers are very conscious about balances, because they can spell the difference between marginal and high-profit loans.

Another mechanism to use in this connection is the rental of money as a compensating balance. Assume again that you want to borrow $5,000. You rent a compensating balance at

1 per cent to 2 per cent. The person providing the "rented" money deposits the $5,000 in a savings account or purchases a certificate of deposit. He collects 4 per cent to 5-1/2 per cent — whatever the going rate is — plus your 1 per cent to 2 per cent. He gets a 5 per cent to 7-1/2 per cent yield. Your cost of the $5,000 you borrow is the bank's interest charge plus the 1 per cent to 2 per cent rental fee. The bank has a 2-1/2 per cent to 4 per cent margin if it lends to you at 8 per cent. Hence, everybody is happy.

You may be able to flush out offsetting deposits (which do what compensating balances do) without paying a compensating balance rental. Hence, if your rich Aunt has $5,000, you may be able to get her to switch banks as a favor. She doesn't lose a penny or take a risk; you get your money; the bank has the higher margin.

FIVE TECHNIQUES FOR BUILDING INCREASING CREDIT

Credit isn't something that you build in an instant. You build your credit over the years and gradually make it evolve into higher borrowing power. It increases with your net worth, your growth performance, and your past credit record. In order to increase your credit and build it consistently, take these five inside steps to a gilt-edged credit reputation:

1. Pay off loans and bills promptly.
2. Build your net worth.
3. Show a pattern of continuing growth.
4. Maintain your personal contacts with loan officers and lending agents.
5. If you're ever forced to withhold payment till after the due date, discuss it with the creditor. Explain why you have to delay and tell him when you will make the payment.

HOW TO GET PAID FOR WHAT
YOU SELL OR LEND

When you sell on credit, you're extending a loan to the buyer. You want to get paid for it. When you lend money to someone else, you want to get repaid. But not everyone pays! In some cases there's no economical legal recourse. In other cases, legal recourse is ineffective because of the debtor's inability to pay. You want to avoid being stuck with bad notes and bad bills. Here are the pitfalls that can cause you to get stuck:

1. Debtor's credit bad
2. Debtor financially incapable
3. Inadequate documentation of transaction
4. Money lent without collateral
5. Improper legal forms used
6. Debtor leaves town
7. Debtor declares bankruptcy
8. Debtor does not have clear title to collateral

In order to avoid these pitfalls and to avoid being stuck with bad debts, investigate the buyer or borrower thoroughly. You can do this by asking for credit references from banks and checking them, or you can go through a credit agency. If there's any doubt about the credit of the buyer or borrower, don't add your name to the list of people that he may stick.

When you sell on credit to someone who is not a charge account customer, use the approved legal chattel mortgage note form that is recognized in your state. If you're lending money on real estate, insist on a properly-drawn-up mortgage note and a title policy or an abstract. Whenever large amounts of money are involved, it's always best to enlist the services of a lawyer.

If you're renting property, do it with the legal lease form that is standard in your state. You can add additional provisions to the so-called "boiler plate," which covers a multitude of eventualities that can arise in a lease situation.

In the lending situation, get collateral that can readily be resold for an amount in excess of the debt. Otherwise, you may find that the value of the collateral is not equal to the value of the debt when you take action on any claim you may have. For example, a car worth $2,500 today may only be worth $1,500 a year from now.

Many businessmen fall down on their collections. When an amount of money is owed to you, pursue the collection aggressively. In a rental situation, never allow a tenant to get behind more than one pay period. They will invariably stick you if you let them get further ahead of you.

Incidentally, you can file a suit for collection in small claims courts in most states without a lawyer and with a very low filing fee. There's a top limit to the amount of the suit ($200 to $500 in most states). If you can keep your credit sales in small enough amounts to take collection actions in small claims courts, you'll usually save yourself expense and headaches.

SYNDICATES, JOINT VENTURES, AND CORPORATIONS SIMPLIFIED

Syndicates and joint ventures may or may not be incorporated. The members of the syndicate or joint venture may be individuals or corporations. Generally, a group of individuals joined together in a specific venture is called a "syndicate." The joint venture terminology is generally used when the participants in the venture are corporations. The purpose of the syndicate is to raise a larger amount of money than a single individual can readily raise, and to minimize the risk of each of the individual investors.

For example, ten investors with $10,000 each in a syndicate can purchase raw land, other real property, or a business that requires up to $100,000 in cash. Individually, they might not be able to raise that amount or might not want to take the risk alone.

The person who forms a syndicate sometimes gets participation in the syndicate without investing any money for the effort that he expends in organizing the syndicate and seeing to the syndicate's business. A typical example is the case of a real estate broker friend of mine who forms a syndicate to buy a property that he has listed and gets his sales commission as equity in the syndicate.

Joint ventures are frequently formed by two or more individuals or corporations to enter an ongoing business. The joint venture is usually formed to engage in a new but *continuing* business venture. Thus, a prominent publisher and a computer company have formed a computerized teaching machine company. Ordinarily the joint venture is organized as a corporation, with each of the participants in the venture sharing the stock of the new corporation.

HOW TO FORM YOUR OWN CORPORATION

A corporation has the same status under the law as an individual. The stockholders in the corporation merely own a piece of the corporation, and their liability is generally limited. There are some exceptions to this. The limitation of the liability is usually the amount of stock issued or the cost of the stock issued. Equity in the corporation is easy to transfer, and hence the life of the corporation can be infinite. These features make it possible to attract investors who wish to retain some fluidity while exploiting the benefits of equity growth.

If you decide to incorporate, enlist the services of a lawyer. The cost ranges from approximately $100 to $1,000. In most states you can probably do it for less than $500, including all fees. Here's how you go about forming a corporation and obtaining finances:

Since you're starting the corporation, you are the promoter. Pull your plan together and then prepare some charts to present to potential investors. Include background on inventions, products, the type of businesses, the special characteristics of the concept, and your contribution to the effort. Show the sales potential and your concept for the growth of the corporation.

Next, develop the investment arrangements. Determine how many shares of capital stock will be authorized. Determine how many shares are to be issued to the initial investors and how many you will get for conceiving and promoting the organization. Perhaps you will have a key executive in the organization, or if an invention is involved, an inventor who is entitled to stock.

This information is used to draft an "agreement to organize a corporation." Your lawyer is familiar with this document and can organize it for you. Bear in mind that the more the lawyer knows about the corporation and its plans, the better he'll be able to serve you. He'll also prepare a draft of the "Articles of Incorporation." In addition, you should have a disclosure form for signature by parties to whom you present your proposition. This protects your idea.

When you've secured all of your investors, your lawyer will proceed with the certificate of incorporation, set up minute books, develop tentative by-laws, and go through other essential steps. Then you'll need to hold the first meeting of the incorporators. Elect a board of directors and a chairman and call for payment of the stock subscriptions, and authorize issuance of stock to the subscribers. You'll also have to adopt by-laws and handle other matters which your lawyer and you feel are pertinent. You'll keep minutes of the proceedings of this meeting and of subsequent meetings.

WHERE TO LOOK FOR EQUITY INVESTORS

Equity investors are sometimes difficult to pinpoint. Real estate people generally use the list of professionals (doctors, lawyers, and dentists) as prospects for real estate investments. Professional people generally earn high ordinary incomes and are looking for investments that provide tax advantages, such as capital gains and shelters. The stock of a corporation provides a capital gains opportunity. These same people are reasonably good prospects for your stock subscription. Others who might be interested are known investors, investors who advertise for business opportunities in the classified section of the newspapers, business executives, businessmen, investment companies, and others. You can probably get some leads on potential investors from your banker.

Chapter 7

HOW TO PLAN AND START YOUR PROFITABLE BUSINESS

GET OFF TO A GOOD START

Get off to a good start with your new business regardless of the type of business you plan to enter. In the preceding chapter we've surveyed a number of businesses and business opportunities, and assessed the capital, personal, and other requirements for getting started. But no matter what kind of business you intend to enter, it is important that you get it off to a good start. Get off to a good start by conducting an adequate investigation, planning thoroughly, and then making the plan work in spite of obstacles. In this chapter, I'm going to present a 16-step plan that most smart businessmen follow in choosing and launching a new venture. This is a general plan, and some of the steps may not apply to your specific business. Modify as required to fit your venture.

STEP 1: DEVELOP THE CONCEPT OF YOUR BUSINESS AND STUDY THE FIELD

By this time you've probably converged on the type of business or venture that you want to undertake to start your quest for riches and independence. Some of the steps that will be presented in this chapter may cause you to turn back and reconsider. It's better to make a change before you make a considerable investment in money, time, and other resources, than to make the commitment and then find that you're wrong. The first step to take is to develop the concept of your business and then to study the field. If the field does not look productive, you may have to turn back and try another route.

In what area or areas do you intend to serve?

Bill J., a clerk for a large insurance company, initially decided that he wanted to start an insurance agency. But he went ahead and examined these ten possibilities to see if he ought to consider additional opportunities:

1. Creative/technical (e.g., research, writing, invention, electronic design)
2. Service (e.g., TV repair, janitorial services, motor repair, etc.)
3. Construction (e.g., home building, commercial building, road construction, etc.)
4. Manufacturing (e.g., furniture, bric-a-brac, electronic devices)
5. Selling (e.g., retailing, insurance, wholesaling)
6. Trading (e.g., stock market, commodities, TV sets, air conditioners, tools, factory machines)
7. Finance and investment (e.g., real estate, stocks, businesses, lending)
8. Rentals (e.g., homes, apartments, commercial properties, tools, automotive equipment, machinery)
9. Natural resources (e.g., prospecting, mining, timber, resort properties, etc.)

10. People resources (e.g., secretarial, sales, manufacturing, personnel contracts)

Bill decided to consider these possibilities in addition to the insurance agency opportunity:

Selling — retail (he worked in a men's clothing store after he graduated from high school)

Finance and Investment — real estate (one of his former classmates was doing well in new home sales)

When you've determined this, next determine the special features about your business that will tend to make it more successful than any others in the field. What are the "pluses" that you have to offer?

1. Experience (as a salesman, accountant, manager, plumber, electrician, engineer, artist, or?)
2. Personality (outgoing; salesman-oriented — or ingoing; research, planning-oriented — or handwork, machinery, physical result-oriented)
3. Sincerity (strive to satisfy)
4. Reputation (recognized for a specific capability, such as solving electronics, manufacturing, or insurance requirement problems)
5. Wide acquaintanceship (recognized as a community leader, know all of the people in town, or know all of the people in a specific industry)
6. Large following (lots of people think you're tops in a specific field)
7. Location (downtown, near other businesses of the same kind, easy to find, etc.)
8. Convenience (on the route to many activities, home service, open evenings, or ?)
9. Credit (thirty-day open account, easy credit, or a bank financing plan)
10. Delivery service (daily pick-up and delivery)
11. Fast service (in at 10, out at 4)
12. Economy (low prices, cost discounts)

13. Guarantees (180-day unconditional guaranteed service)
14. Quality (the best, made to last)
15. Easy-pay plan (bank or finance company financing plan)
16. Diverse array of products or services (one-stop service or sales)
17. Higher quality of life (more leisure, less bother, greater comfort)
18. Success (Established 1925, no call-backs in twenty-five years, customer satisfaction for twenty years)

Bill Jackson decided that his experience fitted him for any three of the opportunities he was considering. His experience, personality, sincerity, reputation, and wide acquaintanceship would help him. Since people associated him principally with insurance, he decided his original route was the way to go — but he also decided to work as a real estate agent, since insurance business is associated with property sales. When he checked into the matter of selling real estate, he found he'd have to take out a real estate "salesman's" license and serve under a licensed broker for a year. He found one who would let him sell insurance from his office as well. Hence, Bill ended up with a free office, a ready-made insurance market on the real estate sales of the broker and his other salesmen, and the chance to make real estate sales commissions himself!

What did he stress — besides his experience? One-stop insurance and real estate service.

The list above includes just a few of the possible benefits that might differentiate your business from the other businesses in the pack. These benefits will help to get you off the ground initially and will contribute to your continuing success. You don't have to offer them all, but you must offer at least several of them in order to be different and better.

Now that you've established basic guidelines for the type of business that you're going to enter and the benefits that you'll offer to make your business outstanding, it's time to develop the concept on which you'll operate. In the process of developing this concept, it's important that you study the field of business that you're going to enter with respect to the geographical area that you're going to operate in. Use the classified section of the telephone directory to determine what your competition is, then call on each of these businesses and study them. See what they're offering, how they're offering it, and how you can offer services and what you can do to make your business distinct from those of your competitors. In the process of studying these other businesses and their prospects, you may find that it's unwise to enter the field. Perhaps the field is already overcrowded in your locality, or perhaps one or several of these businesses is so outstandingly good that it will be difficult to establish yours in competition with it. If this is the case, start over.

Assuming that you find a basis to establish the business that you want, determine how you're going to operate, the hours that you're going to be open, the distinct advantages that you'll offer. The several lists that I presented in this section can be helpful.

STEP 2: DETERMINE REAL ESTATE, EQUIPMENT, INVENTORY, EMPLOYEE AND OTHER REQUIREMENTS

Now that you've decided what kind of business you're going to enter, determine what you're going to need in the way of real estate improvements. Are you going to have to be located downtown, or can you operate from your home or a low-traffic location? If manufacturing is your business, you don't need "downtown." If most of your business is done by phone, you don't need "downtown."

Take a look at your equipment requirements. What are you going to need in the way of tools? Machines? Automotive equipment? Handling equipment? Are you going to need any specialized test instruments?

Once you've pinned these things down, take a look at your inventory requirements. How much inventory do you need? Is it $100, $1,000, or $20,000? What kind of variety do you need? Will 10 items do it, or do you need 10,000 items? Where can you obtain the inventory that you need? Locally, in New York, or where? Then, of course, there are the employee requirements. Is it 1, 10, or 100? I would assume that since you are starting a business from scratch, you will probably do a good bit of the work yourself. However, many of the businesses that you might enter will require additional employees. What kind of skills do they need? None, special technical skills, special dexterity, or what? What will you have to pay them? Will it be $2, $3, $5, or? per hour? Can you work with part-time help or will you need full-time help?

What are the other requirements? What about licensing? Are licensing costs high — $5 or $500? Permits? Zoning? Do you have an accountant? A lawyer? Do you have friends who can give you additional ideas on starting your business? Investigate all of these. It's very important that you take them into consideration at this point in your program.

Wally W. decided to go into automotive automatic transmission repairs. He decided to work from a garage in a low rent area (that was zoned business) because most of his business would be by phone in response to yellow page listings and ads, and by referrals from filling stations and general garages which didn't work on transmissions.

He needed $1,000 worth of equipment and $200 worth of inventory. He decided to work as a one-man shop. He found he didn't need any special license, so he was ready for the next step.

STEP 3: DETERMINE THE START-UP COST

Now go back and look over the requirements that you've determined in Steps 1 and 2 of your start-up activity. Then enumerate the start-up costs that you're going to have in your business. You'll have one time only or non-recurring costs that you encounter only when you start up, such as machines, incorporation costs, permits, and initial layout. In addition you'll have recurring overhead costs, such as rent, telephone, advertising, employee costs, office supplies, stationery, rest room and janitorial supplies, and others that are expense items but that are not direct cost items. Take a look, too, at your direct cost items. If you're going to enter the service business, some of your employee costs will be direct costs. If you're going to enter retail, the cost of merchandise is a direct cost. You'll need an initial inventory. Take all of these factors into account and estimate your start-up and operating costs.

Wally W. determined his start-up costs to be $200 for first month's rent, $50 for signs, $50 for utility and phone deposits, and $75 for "grand opening" advertising. Total start-up costs for his transmission shop would be $375. (He considered first month's rent as a start-up cost because he paid it in advance.) His monthly operating costs would be:

Rent	$200
Phone	30
Advertising	50
Utilities	30
Office Supplies and Misc.	20
Monthly Operating Expense	$330

STEP 4: MAKE A MARKET SURVEY

Make a market survey of the businesses in your area that will be competitive with you. You've already become familiar with these businesses during the course of your earlier activity. You can accomplish some of the information-gathering tasks on this step concurrently with Step 1. Determine the locations of businesses that will be competitive with you. Observe the traffic that they have, the business that they have, and then walk into the store or the service establishment, whatever it is, and get a feel for the way they do business, the way they treat customers. Be prepared to ask about a specific product or a specific service in order to get a feel for the way they operate.

After leaving the store, make notes of your impressions of the store or the service business or whatever it may be; after you have completed making the rounds of all of those in your locality, put your information together. Determine whether there is room for a new competitor in this field. Work the business from the other end, too. Talk to friends and neighbors and determine their feelings about the needs for the products or services that are involved.

You don't have to make the kind of sophisticated, formal market survey the big companies make. Such a formal market survey involves considerably more effort than the value of the result produced. But you'll find that the simplified type of market survey that I've talked about is essential. You can make additional comparisons by comparing the statistics on businesses in your locality against businesses in other localities.

Wally W. checked his locality for other transmission shops. There wasn't one within three miles of his location, and the shop in the adjoining neighborhood had more work than it could handle. This competitor took in about ten jobs a day, and more work was going to other shops located farther away.

STEP 5: DETERMINE YOUR SHARE OF THE MARKET

Determine your share of the market. Estimate the total market for the product or service that is to be offered in your community in terms of dollars to be spent annually. Then, discounting the lesser businesses, determine the number of businesses in the specific activity that you're going to enter and add one (for yourself) to this quantity. Divide this quantity into the total dollar market. See if there's enough for you to make a profit and a living. Wally W. did this in a relatively simple manner.

Wally W. figured he could get five transmission jobs a day after looking over the competitive situation. He figured he could only handle three jobs a day working by himself. At an average of $100 each for three jobs, he figured he'd be taking in $300 a day.

The superb optimist always believes he can get more than his share of the market. The supreme pessimist always believes that he will get less than his share of the market. At this point, it becomes a point of human judgment. You're on your own; decide whether or not you can make it with the portion of the market that you feel you can get.

STEP 6: PREPARE A CASH FLOW PROJECTION

Your cash flow projection is an estimate of the revenues that your business will receive and the portion of it that you will retain as spendable cash. The cash flow projection follows the outline shown in Figure 1. Lay it out either on a weekly or monthly basis. Then start to fill in the numbers. This will give you a feel for the amount of money that you can expect to take in, the amount of money that you'll have to expend in pursuing your business, and the amount of money that you can pull out of the business as spendable cash. You start by entering the revenue indicated by your market survey. Then pick up the costs that you will have in the conduct of your business as developed in Step 3. When you come up with a positive cash flow at the end of the week or the month, you've cash that you can carry forward. If you come up with a negative cash flow, it is essential that you have funds available either in reserve or through borrowing power to cover the deficit. Go through several cash flow projections. It may take several before you come up with a plan that is feasible and acceptable. Bear this in mind: It's more productive to do this on paper than to do it with money if it's a losing proposition. If it shows up as a winning proposition on paper, then the trick is to convert it into a winning proposition with dollars.

Wally W.'s projection based on monthly operation (25 business days) is shown in Figure 1. He used his start-up cost ($375) as item 13 for the first period.

Wally decided that he might have been over-optimistic about the market, but his figures assured him that the potential was there.

STEP 7: ANALYZE THE RESULTS OF THE FIRST SEVEN STEPS

Now sit back and take stock of the seven steps that you've just gone through. Does it still seem wise to enter the business that you've planned on? Are there some changes that you'll have to make if the business is feasible? Are there some changes which you'll have to make in order to make the business run more smoothly? What can you do to improve it? These are questions that you'll have to ask your-

CASH FLOW PROJECTION

	Period 1	Period 2	Period — —
1. Total Income	$7,500		
2. Purchases	1,500		
3. Gross Profit (1—2)	6,000		
4. Rent	200		
5. Utilities	30		
6. Phone	30		
7. Advertising	50		
8. Office Supplies	20		

9.	Salaries and Wages	0
10.	Other Over-head	0
11.	Overhead (sum through 10)	330
12.	Net Profit (loss) (3—11)	5,670
13.	Cash (14 preceding period)	(375)
14.	Current Cash (need) (12—13)	5,295

Figure 1

self and available counsel. If it still appears to be feasible for you to continue, then move on to the next step. If it appears that the proposition that you've selected is a marginal one, then start over at Step 1 with a new business idea.

STEP 8: SEEK DISINTERESTED COUNSEL

Up to this time, you've done most of the work yourself. You have here and there relied on the counsel of friends and acquaintances. At this point it is highly desirable to enlist the counsel of quite a few people. Talk to accountants, lawyers, people who are in the same business in other localities who would not be competitive with you, the Small Business Administration, and other government agencies. Ask them for ideas and opinions on your new venture. Your friends and associates are additional sources of counsel. Discuss your plans with them and evaluate their comments.

If you enlist the counsel of an expert, follow his advice to the letter; otherwise you're spending your money for naught. But don't confuse the quarterbacking of an *inexpe-*

rienced friend with that of *experienced counsel!* An inexperienced friend *may* produce an idea. An expert can produce sound knowledge!

STEP 9: OBTAIN FINANCING AND DETERMINE EQUIPMENT AND INVENTORY DELIVERY POSSIBILITIES

At this point, you're set to get started on your business. Some of the steps which follow this one may have to be implemented in advance of this step, depending on the kind of business you are going to enter. Before you can obtain financing, you've got to pin down costs in detail. For example, if you're going into the rug-cleaning business, contact the suppliers of rug-cleaning equipment and supplies. Determine the prices, and determine the delivery dates that you can expect. From this you can go back and obtain firm financing requirement figures.

The next step is to take your financing requirements to your bank or to some other lending institution and obtain the financing that you'll need to get started in the business if your own funds are inadequate. Chapter Six, which is devoted to financial strategy, should be reviewed for guidance in obtaining financing.

STEP 10: FIND A BUILDING OR SPACE FOR THE BUSINESS

Your next step is to find a building or space for your business. In some instances you will have to determine this before you can go to the bank. You can firm this up with an option to lease or purchase the specific property that you're going to need.

If you're going to rent the place in which you're going to do business, you'll generally have to lease the property. The lease is a two-way street because it protects you by assuring you that the location will be available to you for a specified time at a specified price. It protects the owner or lessor in that he can rely on your occupancy of the space for a given time. I would caution against going into a month-to-month situation unless business conditions are sufficiently static or you know the owner of the property sufficiently well that you will not be ejected when he has an opportunity to lease at a better price or on a longer term basis. On the other hand, if you can obtain your location on a month-to-month basis with this kind of assurance, you limit your liability.

Bert F. rented an old house for use as an antique store on a month-to-month basis. The house was to be torn down sometime between a year and fifteen months after he moved into it. Hence, he felt reasonably sure that he could establish his business and build mailing lists to bring the business he built to a new location within a year. A year later he had to move, but his business survived and prospered. On the other hand, Albert Smith, an appliance repair man, moved into a run-down location seven years ago on a month-to-month basis. He's still there. The building has been improved and his rent has gone up, but he's still getting a bargain!

STEP 11: PLACE EQUIPMENT AND INVENTORY ORDERS

You may possibly have already placed orders for equipment and inventory. If you haven't, now is the time to do it. If you have, now is the time to firm up the address and the time of delivery. Keep good records as you go along so that you won't lose track of important details such as this one.

STEP 12: RECRUIT EMPLOYEES

If you require employees in the conduct of your business, begin your recruiting activities. Start with classified advertisements and by contacting people that you know who

might be interested in your employment. Here are some of
the characteristics that you'll be interested in looking for in
the prospective employees that you interview:

1. Honesty
2. Integrity
3. Skill
4. Experience
5. Loyalty
6. Personality
7. Appearance
8. Attitude
9. Verbal skills
10. Written skills
11. Neatness
12. Courage
13. Courtesy

There are a number of other things that you will want to
look for in employees, too. Bear in mind that you can't get
miracle workers and supermen at lowest wages. You may
have to pay more to get the kind of employee you desire.
Willard O., for example, started a machine shop. He had
to pay $5.00 an hour to get a skilled machinist, but his other
shop helpers work for $2.00 to $2.50 an hour.

STEP 13: PREPARE OPENING
PROMOTION CAMPAIGN

The ultimate success of any business is influenced by the
starting promotion and first impression that the business
presents to the community. So plan on an adequate and outstanding initial opening promotion campaign, as well as an
unusual opening day event. Search for novel ways to make
the existence of the business known to the community.
Develop community interest with heavy advertising, door
prizes, imprinted give-aways (such as ball point pens), a

large host-hostess team, and other devices that prevent opening fizzles. You can't get business unless people know that you are in business, where you're located, and how to get in touch with you. This is one of the purposes of an opening promotion campaign. So don't skimp on advertising. The next chapter contains a number of successful techniques on promotion and salesmanship to help you through a successful opening promotion for your business.

I applied the heavy advertising, door prizes, discounts on opening days, and low-cost "leaders" techniques to opening one of my own businesses. I had over 1000 people in two days in an area of town where people seldom went to buy!

STEP 14: OBTAIN LICENSES AND PERMITS REQUIRED

Not everything about a new business is fun, and one of the non-fun things about starting a new business is that you become involved in a number of licenses, permits, and tax-collection duties for various government entities. You're subject to legal and zoning restrictions that make the chore of running a business less than fun. You have to get phones and utilities connected, too.

To determine local licensing requirements, make a trip or phone call to city hall prior to your visit. County requirements are frequently tied in with city and state requirements. In many states there's a sales tax. You can generally find the appropriate office listed under the name of your state in the telephone directory. You may work with the controller's office, the tax service office, or some similar title in handling sales tax and other state requirements.

If you're in special businesses which involve federal and state agencies over and beyond ordinary taxing agencies, you'll have to check into these as well. This pertains particularly to food and drugs.

STEP 15: EQUIP AND STOCK THE BUSINESS

Your equipment and your inventory should be arriving at this stage of the game. Install your fixtures and equipment. Then stock your shelves with inventory and start up any processes that may be involved in addition. For example, if we're talking about retail, it's simply a matter of putting up the shelves and fixtures, pricing the merchandise, stocking the shelves, and instructing your personnel. If we're talking about a wholesale business, you'll want to get your sales people out on the road and start to get the orders rolling in. If it's a manufacturing business, you'll want to get your training for production underway. This step should include completely equipping and stocking the business and getting it going.

STEP 16: OPEN FOR BUSINESS

At this point your employees are all trained and you're ready to do business. You will probably have lost several pounds and several nights' sleep by this time, but you will probably also still be buoyed on by your enthusiasm for your new business. In the days, weeks, and months that lie ahead of you, you'll encounter numerous challenges and discouragements, and sometimes the weight and responsibility of being a businessman will almost overwhelm you. Nevertheless, keep this in mind: The determined individual who decides what he's going to do and decides to go ahead and do it in spite of all, always manages to accomplish his objectives. Here are some more thoughts on the subject.

WHAT MAKES PEOPLE SUCCEED IN BUSINESS

There are definite and specific characteristics that you can develop to enhance your chances of success in business, and for that matter, in any endeavor. We're not going into a long discourse on them in this chapter, but I'd like to list briefly the techniques the pros use to develop themselves. If you have or develop these traits to their fullest, your success and mounting wealth will probably surpass your wildest dream. You'll notice, incidentally, that many of these traits have been brought into play in earlier chapters of this book.

1. Develop your desire for success and wealth
2. Be determined to get what you want
3. Have faith that you can do it
4. Meet uncertainty with courage
5. Make firm decisions on courses of action
6. Enter each task with enthusiasm
7. Use your imagination to dream new dreams
8. Develop vision to foresee the future
9. Employ perspective to gauge relative importance
10. Bounce back in the face of discouragement

Here are eight more important action areas for optimum success in business:

1. Develop creativity and mental agility to forge new plans and ideas and redirect astray plans
2. Be practical; realize what is possible and what isn't
3. Organize and develop method to make "it" work
4. Give your clients and customers service that makes them want to return for more
5. Plan and schedule your action to realization
6. Show kindness and courtesy to win enduring friends
7. Have the vitality, health and temperament to go the long mile by developing good habits
8. Control direction to keep your program on the path to success.

Chapter 8

TECHNIQUES THAT KEEP THE
CASH ROLLING IN

BLAKE L. TRIPLED HIS INCOME
IN THREE MONTHS

Blake L. was earning $5,000 a year as a maintenance man at Harvard University. During his lifetime, he'd never earned more than this. A few years before he reached retirement age he suddenly quit, went into the real estate business, and within three months had tripled his income. Think of it! He worked a lifetime for a low salary. Then all of a sudden he pitched his retirement and tripled his income!

How did he do it? He did it by selling. He learned how to make a property attractive through an effective sales presentation. He learned how to find products (properties) to sell, how to find prospects to buy, and how to make the two match.

Whether you get into a business that is a fundamental sales business or into a less sales-oriented business, such as a service business, the basic requirement for salesmanship remains. This chapter will make you a better salesman, advertiser and promoter so that you can keep the cash rolling in and put profits in your pocket.

GOOD SALESMANSHIP SPELLS PROFIT IN ANY BUSINESS

Salesmanship can mean the difference between failure and success in any business. No matter how well you manage your business, it can't succeed unless you sell. It takes good salesmanship to make a business succeed in spite of everything else. The value of salesmanship is apparent when you realize that there are more salesmen making $40,000 or more a year than there are doctors. Yet a doctor spends years in college and medical school and a salesman doesn't have to take special training. Good salesmen make more than good engineers, accountants, managers, administrators. Even in these professions the pay is higher if the individual professional is also a good salesman. With the value of salesmanship so high, isn't it obvious that you ought to develop and cultivate yourself as a salesman to succeed in your business?

Salesmanship begins with the head man. If you're a good salesman, you'll emphasize salesmanship in all of your activities; consequently, your employees will respect sales ability and try to develop it in themselves. *Good salesmanship spells profit in any business, so write it into yours.*

SIX WAYS TO CONVERT TIMID, UNCOLORFUL PEOPLE INTO TOP SALESMEN

These are the six things it takes to develop yourself or your employees into top sales people:

1. Study
2. Actual selling experience
3. Confidence
4. Enthusiasm
5. Common sense
6. A reasonable effort

So how do you get these things going? First of all, *begin with a thorough study of salesmanship in books that you can obtain from the library,* and *while you are at it, study advertising techniques and speaking.* Learn as much as you can about these things. Then dig into books on *psychology* to get a better feel for what makes people do things.

Second, *acquire experience and practice by actually trying to sell.* After you've gone through several sales situations with some successes and perhaps some failures, you'll have a much better feel for the whole field of selling. You may find that your confidence wilts just a little bit with some of the no's that you'll receive.

So take the third step: *Build your confidence* in yourself and in other people. If necessary, *talk to the mirror till you're sure that you've got your sales pitch well in hand* and that you feel sure you make a decent presentation.

If you don't have enthusiasm for your selling and for your product, you can't do anything. So take time out for the fourth step! *Get excited about your product!* Develop better and better sales pitches, more and more selling points for your product.

Fifth, *use common sense* in *prospecting* for customers, in *organizing* your sales itinerary, in *making your presentations,* and in *dealing with people.* When you do these things, you'll find that you're utilizing your time much more productively and your sales will go up. Of course, if you're selling in a store, your prospecting turns into a matter of getting people into your place of business. Your sales itinerary then becomes a matter of being available in the store to sell. Put common sense into the whole works.

Sixth, *put a reasonable effort into your selling*. If you tend to let yourself be occupied too much with other matters and feel that customers are interfering with what you are trying to get done, the chances are that you'll put very little selling effort into your day. Remember, the primary thing is to sell and to move merchandise. Furthermore, *don't quit for the day because things aren't going well or because you haven't sold enough.* You might sell the whole store at two minutes after five o'clock!

DEVELOP SELLING POINTS
FOR YOUR PRODUCT

In determining selling points for your product, consider these parameters:

1. Style (It's the latest thing. Everybody who's important is wearing it.)
2. Design (Notice the rounded corners designed for extra safety.)
3. Kind of Material (This is a *pure* silk tie.)
4. Finish (This table has a lifetime Eterna-Gloss top.)
5. Construction (This car has a welded lifetime frame.)
6. Quality of Construction (This hi-fi features gold plated circuit boards.)
7. Uniqueness (This Swiss chalet house is unique inside and out.)
8. Durability (The motor in this saw is guaranteed for ten years.)
9. Value versus cost (Worth $10, it costs only $4.98 today.)
10. Comfort (This air conditioner will keep you cool when everyone else is sweltering.)
11. Beauty (Lovely tree-filled home lots like this one are getting scarce.)

12. Utility (Do you know of any other kitchen appliance that will do so many things?)

You can build this list depending on the type of product that you have. These are the things to keep in mind whenever you're building a sales pitch, whenever you're attempting to answer and field objections, whenever you're in a selling situation, and whenever you're writing an ad.

SIX STEPS TO MAKING A SALE

There are six steps to making a sale. Here they are!

Step 1. Break the prospect's preoccupation. Catch his attention.

Step 2. Appeal to his emotions and desire for personal benefit. Make his desire grow.

Step 3. Build value. Show him that the value is far greater than the cost.

Step 4. Ask committing questions and make the customer participate in selling himself. Make him say, "Yes — Yes — Yes."

Step 5. Present proof that builds the customers's confidence and influences his judgment.

Step 6. Close. Show the customer why he should buy today and be ready with clinchers.

HOW TO GET ATTENTION
AND BREAK PREOCCUPATION

If your prospect is preoccupied with his hobby, a problem, a conference with a business associate or another salesman, or has another matter on his mind, you may do well to see him at another time. A great interrupter is not a great salesman. Likewise, in the retail situation when a customer enters your store and begins to talk about a non-business matter, follow through with him. If you interrupt, you may damage your chances for a sale.

There are times when you call on a man when he is not busy and is involved with work that can be accomplished at any time. In this case you're not interrupting a labor of love, but you may have to still compete against routine for the man's time. So how do you attract attention? Break his pre-occupation; sweep his mind clean for your presentation or proposition. Here's how: "You can increase your profit two to five times with this advertising program," or "You can save $3,000 per year with this program." Never ask a man if he has time to see you; get right into it. You have a head start if you get right to the point.

THE WAY TO CREATE DESIRE TO BUY

We have emotions that motivate us to respond with attention. If they're excited, our desire grows, and we're motivated to action. These emotions include:

1. Desire for recognition, prestige, publicity, and other forms of attention. This emotional response results from appeal to the ego. "You'll be the best dressed man in town," or "People respect a man with the knowledge this book imparts."

2. Desire for safety, health, well-being, and shelter. The stimulation of this response by arousing fear of consequences is a secondary approach to this emotion. "You wouldn't want to endanger your family to save $50 on a heating system."

3. Desire for wealth, improved standard of living, and increased savings is sometimes called the material, acquisition, or profit emotion. "What's in it for me?" is the question that an appeal to this emotion answers. "This store location will double your sales and profits."

4. Romantic emotion is a world apart from the others be-cause it involves the desire to do things that are out of the ordinary for the individual prospect. Typical key words in

appealing to this emotion are: "Imagine yourself   ."
Or, "Wouldn't it be wonderful to   ?"

5. Sex emotion involves the desire to be attractive to the opposite sex and to establish a home and a family. Cosmetics and clothing advertisements have sales appeals that aim for this target. "With Lady X perfume, men will always notice you."

The sex emotion is an extension of the romance classification, but it has a distinct element that classifies it for a separate listing. An appeal to romance does not necessarily involve the other sex. A romantic thing is an out-of-the-ordinary thing. It may be a dream today and a possible reality in the future.

You can probably expand this list of emotions to which sales appeals can be made. Here are some more examples.

The desire for recognition might include an appeal like, "Only a man of your outstanding leadership ability can function as our local distributor." The emotion of self-preservation and well-being can be stimulated by appeals like, "You want to have a washing machine that's guaranteed by a reliable manufacturer, don't you?" The desire for profit and savings may respond to appeals like this: "Would you like to save $10,000 a year on your truck operations?" or "If you could double your sales through this program, wouldn't your profits increase?" The romantic emotion might be capped with: "Now, Mr. Jones, you and your wife can enjoy the pleasures of a Caribbean vacation" or "Picture yourself at the wheel of a new Ford convertible, riding as smoothly as a mystic on a magic carpet during the golden autumn." (Don't get carried away on this romance bit, though!)

HOW TO MAKE THE PROSPECT
HELP TO SELL HIMSELF

The prospect will help to sell himself if you get him involved and have him participate in the actual selling experience. One way to do this is to ask the prospect committing questions as you continue through your sales pitch.

For example, "You'd like to save $300 a year on your eating, wouldn't you, Mr. Jones?" Make him say, "Yes." Another point: Use his name frequently in order to build empathy. This way he tends to become more involved and to participate more actively in the sale. Each time you get him to say, "Yes," you come closer to getting him to say "Yes" when you ask for the order. The oftener you use his name, the more familiar he feels toward you.

HOW TO PYRAMID THE PRODUCT VALUE IN THE PROSPECT'S MIND

Everybody likes a bargain, so build the value. Tell your prospect that you're giving him a bargain. You don't have to reduce the price or resort to expensive premiums. You don't have to cheapen your image to give the prospect a bargain that will result in a sale. Simply build the value.

Here are several phrases that you can use to build the value of a product: "Saves you a hundred dollars a year — costs only $29.95." "Was $20.00; this week only $9.95." "Worth $10.00; only $7.95." "Buy this car for $1795 before prices go up." "Thousands have paid $30 for this razor — our price is $24.95." "Handcrafted furniture at new, low budget prices."

You don't always have to become involved in price to build the value. Words such as "executive," "handcrafted," "custom-made," and "luxurious" connote value. When you're dealing with prices, play on the fact that prices were higher, that they're going up, that the value of the product exceeds the price, that the product saves more than the price, or compare it to a similar product that costs more.

PROOF AND CONFIDENCE BUILDING
THAT CLINCHES SALES

Sometimes you can move right on to the "close" from the preceding step, but you may have to present proof before you do that. Proof can take many forms: User testimonials, financial statements, magazine articles, guarantees, or other documentation provide the proof required to convince the customer that his judgment is good — that he is doing what other smart people are doing. Here are some typical proof and confidence building statements:

1. Testimonials ("Mr. Jones says") ("Mr. Jones endorses")
2. Approval statements ("Approved by Underwriter Laboratories")
3. List of famous customers
4. Long success statements ("Founded in 1920") ("50 Years of Continuous Service")
5. Test results ("20 per cent fewer cavities")
6. Expert testimony ("Dr. Jones, recognized authority, says,   ")
7. Statistics ("Four out of five automobile accident deaths can be avoided with seat belts.")
8. Brand product names ("General Electric," "General Motors," "Ford")
9. Guarantees ("Money-back guarantee") ("Three-year warranty")
10. Proved product popularity ("70 per cent of all cars are General Motors products")

THE STEP THAT POOR SALESMEN FORGET

The step that poor salesmen forget is to close the sale; that is, to get a signed order or to take the cash and wrap the merchandise — and this, of course, makes all the difference. After you've taken the prospective customer through the five steps leading to the close, you've built his interest from some relatively low level to a higher one. You build interest till you feel that it is high enough to cause the prospect to buy, then you go after the close.

Diplomatic closes are, "Please check whether you want the blue or the black," as you pass the pencil. After he's checked the blank, he'll usually sign the line that you've singled out with a big X without another word. If he doesn't, ask, "Did I mark your signature line?" or getting more direct, "Please check the order as I've written it and if it's correct, please sign it." Or ask, "Shall I gift wrap it?" or, "Shall I carry it to your car?"

"Do you prefer to pay cash or to budget the payments?" leads to the close, and "Shall I write this up for the twelve month plan or the eighteen month plan?" gets right to the point.

When you get to the closing point, you should be ready with a reason to buy. You may get to close without using proof, but you may need the reason to buy now to clinch your closing. "Buy now to avoid the rush and depleted stocks." "Buy now to take advantage of this special introductory offer," or "Buy now to assure installation before winter," etc.

Use "Prices are always going up," or "We've reduced the price for a limited time only," or "Start to realize the savings now — it costs you $10 each day you're without it," and similar reasons to buy now.

There are plenty of ways to close the sale, and there are plenty of ways to lose it. When you've closed the sale, leave or excuse yourself to wait on another customer. Even after you've closed it, you may lose it although the man has signed or paid. As long as the customer is still talking to you, he can change his mind and may not consider the transaction closed. If you or he walk away, the transaction is completed. He's less likely to change his mind!

You may have to be ready with a "clincher." You work the customer toward the close. He's nearly ready to buy, but he needs an additional inducement. Your reason to buy now may do the trick, or the customer may state a condition to the sale. Your response should be, "I'm not sure that we can do it, but if you'll sign this order subject to approval by my management, I'll try to help you get it through." The sale will usually be made. If the customer doesn't want to sign but says he'll buy if his conditions are met, try this:

"But Mr. Jones, I cannot get my management to act on a request of this sort unless I have a firm proposal to present."

So, there you have them: Six steps in the science of making a sale.

HANDLING OBJECTIONS

The good salesman fields objections aptly and turns them into reasons for buying. Here are some typical objections (o) and the counters (c).

1. (o) "Business is bad."
   (c) "With this program you'll make your business get better."
2. (o) "Business is good."
   (c) "Yes, and that's all the more reason why you should be working to make it better, so you'll have a firm base when prosperity drops off."
3. (o) "But I don't need it now."
   (c) "Yes, but by working with it now, you'll be ready to use it when you need it."
4. (o) "I don't need it now."
   (c) "Prices are going up. You'll save by buying it now."
5. (o) "Business is good."
   (c) "That means it will cost you less now, since

your income tax is higher. It's a deductible business expense."

6. (o) "It costs too much."
   (c) "Not at all. It will pay for itself five to twenty times over in the first year."

7. (o) "I don't like the color."
   (c) "Do you prefer brown, red, or gray?"

8. (o) "It's too big."
   (c) "You'd rather have a ruggedly built quality product than a flimsy one that will fall apart, wouldn't you?"

9. (o) "My utility bills are too high already."
   (c) "But this air conditioner will increase sales and more than pay for itself.

10. (o) "I can't afford it now."
    (c) "Prices are going up on everything. It will cost more in the future."

HOW TO SYNTHESIZE
YOUR BUSINESS IMAGE

Every business, whether it likes it or not, has an image or a number of images. Although you like to think of the image of your business as being your property, it really isn't. It's something that exists in people's minds, and every mind may have a different image of your business. However, you will want to take steps to shape that image in people's minds to conform to what you want it to be. Here are some of the characteristics that you can incorporate into the image you attempt to build for your business.

1. Quality
2. Guaranteed satisfaction
3. Fast service
4. Folksiness
5. Sophistication

6. Public-minded spirit
7. Considerate treatment
8. Technically outstanding performance
9. Firmly established business

Some of these image connotations are contradictory, and you can't choose them all for your business. After giving the matter a little thought, you may find an image or combination that suits you on this list, or you may come up with some other ideas that you want to incorporate in the image that you project for your business. Once you've chosen the image that you believe best, the next thing is to begin to project it.

To project your image you'll have to look at all facets of your business, including promotion, advertising, personnel and the way they deal with customers, the interior of the store, including layout, fixtures, and decoration, and any number of other things. All of these things help to shape an image, so you'll have to consider all of them.

PROMOTION PLANS THAT BUILD THE IMAGE

Promotion plans help to build the image of a business. If you promote with flashy circulars and stress low prices, you'll build an image as a bargain house or as a cheap store. On the other hand, if you promote with attractive and sophisticated brochures, you'll suggest a sophisticated, quality image. You can suggest folksiness, too, by going a middle-of-the-road promotion without any drastic price reduction.

Richard L. operates a gas station. He picked a smiling face caricature (long before "smile" buttons) as his trademark. His trademark and the slogan "Richard's Smiling Service" appears on a sign in front of his station and on his ads and circulars. All of his employees give the customers a smile. His image — friendliness.

FOOLPROOF BUSINESS OPENING
PROMOTION TECHNIQUES

When you're going to open a new business, plan an event for the opening. Plan this event well in advance of the actual date on which it is to happen. Then set up an advertising campaign to promote the opening in your local newspaper, through circulars, telephone calls, mailings, and possibly on radio and TV. Promote the opening thoroughly, but remember that you've got to plan the opening promotion before you *promote* the promotion.

At your opening, you will want to show off your place of business and you will want those who come to the opening to meet your personnel. Everybody should put their best foot forward at this event. You can get something new and special to show (in addition to the merchandise that you have on hand) from one of your suppliers. Possibly he'll even send some of his personnel to help you in the opening. You may wish to make refreshments available at your opening, as one novelty company did. They also had balloons for the children and a useful gadget for grown-ups. Possibly an advertising-type gratuity, such as a telephone book cover or a ballpoint pen with your imprint, address and phone number to make people appreciate and remember you might help.

You'll want to be sure that you have your sign placed for the opening. The novelty company mentioned before had a drawing with door prizes. You might do the same, run a contest, or you might be able to have a celebrity present for the opening. Football players are popular for openings around Dallas.

For your opening promotion, seek ways to make people want to come out. Prepare for the opening so that it will be an enjoyable and pleasant event that comes off without a hitch. If you can make all of these things work together, there's no doubt about it: People will know where you are, what kind of business you are in, and you'll establish some good will and a following for your business right at the outset.

HOW TO WRITE ADS THAT SELL

Your advertising cost is the same whether your ads are effective or whether they are ineffective. You pay for space, but the thing that makes an ad succeed is the copy. The first thing is to attract attention. Photographs or a drawing will help to attract attention to a display ad. In a classified ad, your headline is the only thing that you have to attract attention. Whether the ad is classified or display, headlines attract readership. Make your headline good. Address the particular audience that you want. For example, newspapers seeking newsboys to deliver newspapers always start their ads off with: "Boys, make money!" (Or something of that sort.) Address your audience in your headline. Give the ad some punch by including a benefit. Your address to a specific audience might include any of the following:

Men, Women, Ladies, Boys, Girls, Young Misses, House-wives, Mothers, Executives, Professional Men, Homeowners, Young Couples, Young Families, Mature Men. These, of course, are not all-inclusive.

There are some words that advertising experts recognize as good attention-getters. Here are a few of the better ones: New, Latest, New Discovery, Amazing, Remarkable, Magic, Miracle, How-To, Easy, Free, Guaranteed, Special Offer, Introducing, Reward. Try to get one or more of these words in the headline.

Here are some specific benefits that you might consider to make your headlines offer specific benefits:

1. Earn $12,000 a year or more for your services
2. $85.00 suits, now only $49.00
3. You can borrow $300 today.
4. Europe — $371 for fourteen days

Notice that each of these headlines offers a specific benefit.

The body copy of your ad follows the points in making the sale that we've discussed in connection with salesmanship. Use your body copy to do the following:

1. Build the value
2. Establish confidence
3. Make it easy to buy
4. Make your store easy to find
5. Inspire an immediate purchase
6. Reward the reader

You can reward the reader by making your ad enjoyable to read. This can sometimes be done by inserting some local color in your advertising, or by including news of a local event.

Try to get position that is advantageous to your ad. The right-hand page of a newspaper is generally more effective than the left-hand page. The size you choose may have something to do with the position that you can get. For example, a three column by ten inch ad will usually stand out on a page because it will usually start out at the top of the page. Even if it doesn't, it kills the chances of a half-page ad being in conflict with yours. Generally there would be some news printed at the top of the page.

HOW TO GET FREE PUBLICITY

You can get free publicity through news stories in the daily press, trade newspapers and magazines, house publications, and on radio and TV. There are plenty of things about your business that you can use to make news. Right at the outset, get newspaper coverage of your opening. Although you may have some problems in placing some types of publicity due to the advertising conflict and the pressure on publications to publicize businesses, you can still get some things through.

Here are some things that make news:

1. New products
2. New processes
3. New facilities
4. Management changes
5. Expansion
6. Outstanding outside accomplishments by management or employee personnel
7. Written articles by employees
8. New, enlarged contract
9. Visit by important person

You'll be more likely to get publicity if you write up the article and present it to the newspaper in final form. Small town newspapers with small staffs will generally respond to this kind of a release more readily than a large town newspaper, but even the larger newspaper will appreciate receiving a concise statement of the facts if it is going to do a story on the particular thing that you wish to publicize.

The salesmanship techniques, the promotion know-how, and the advertising tips that have been presented in this chapter will help you to sell. Sales are what make businesses prosper and grow. Don't ever forget it.

Chapter 9

TACTICS THAT SAVE MONEY
AND MAXIMIZE PROFIT

PROFIT IS WHAT YOU KEEP

In business, profit is what you keep. It's the difference between the money you take in and the money that you spend on merchandise and expenses. The optimizing strategies are:

1. Sell high;
2. Buy low;
3. Reduce expenses to zero.

While this represents the ultimate, it is hardly realistic. Competition will tend to set the upper limits on the price that you demand, but you'll discover ways to beat this constraint in the next section.

Your supplier's cost and the level of competition in his field will influence what merchandise or raw materials cost you, but you can beat this constraint, too, with some of the strategies you'll learn in this chapter. You'll learn how to get the highest price, buy for less, and cut expenses to the bone in this chapter.

SELL OR TRADE FOR
THE HIGHEST PRICE

Whenever you sell or trade a business, a product, or a service, command the highest price possible. There are several strategies that make it possible for you to receive the highest price. These strategies are:

1. Develop to highest value
2. Finance a portion of the sale
3. Sell to a group
4. Get competing bidders
5. Add a bonus
6. Refinance to get a higher price

To develop his business to its highest value, Bob R. increased the sales and the profits. To improve a house he owned to its highest value, Kerry L. dressed the property up and raised the rent (and hence the income). To convert a used desk to its highest value, a friend of mine repairs, paints, and makes it more attractive. To make his plumbing service have the highest possible value, Bill S. does the job well and guarantees his work. Make performance and customer satisfaction the primary objective. Deal professionally and courteously with the customer.

Jay H. *increases value by financing a portion of the sale* and giving concessions in down payment. He still gets the full asking price. He simply lowers the amount of cash that he gets when he sells the product. His prospect may buy a vacuum cleaner for $10 down, but skip it at $100 cash. Of course, the buyer's credit has to be good. There's no point in selling if there's doubt about getting paid.

To receive the highest value for a high-ticket item such as real estate, an airplane or a boat, sell to a group. Willard H.

works this way in syndicating real estate. While one member of the group individually may not be able to afford the product, the group, by pooling its resources, may raise a substantial down payment and be able to meet the payments as they fall due.

Up the value of a business, real estate, or a product *by getting competing bidders.* A top Dallas moneymaker sells all of his properties by auction. A prospective buyer who really wants a car you have to sell will move a lot faster if he feels that someone is bidding against him.

Add a bonus as a clincher to sell if necessary. The bonus may take the form of a discount, a free accessory, or a related product. For example, "I'll throw in a free dado set if you'll buy this table saw today," is a typical clincher of a hardware store.

If you own a high equity in a business, real estate, or a product, refinance it to get a higher price when you sell. This gives you full cash but lowers the down payment for the buyer. There's another aspect to this, too. You get your name off the note, and the entire responsibility for collection falls on the lender.

BUY AT ROCK BOTTOM PRICES

Buy at rock bottom prices. Jay O. brings down the purchase cost by buying in quantity, by playing off one supplier against another, and by taking advantage of unusual purchasing opportunities. Keep your eye open for failing businesses, fire sales, damaged merchandise, and even "leaders" that big stores sell below cost. (One resourceful dealer had five buyers accumulating $15 appliances offered "one to a customer" at $5.98. Wholesale cost to him would have been around $9!) The classifieds sometimes contain fantastic bargains. Watch these, too!

In Chapter Ten you'll be introduced to techniques for buying businesses and properties at rock bottom prices. Now let's look at ways to cut operating expenses to the bone and still convey the image of a big-time operation.

SAVE $300 to $1000 A MONTH ON LOCATION

You can save a considerable amount of money by locating your business in your home. You will save on rent, on utilities, on the telephone, and if your wife can answer the phone for you, on employees. Many businesses have been started from homes — but bear in mind that if you take this approach, you lose the benefits of location for a business that relies on walk-in "traffic."

"FRONT" TACTICS THAT WILL PUT YOUR HOME BUSINESS UPTOWN

You can overcome some of the "small-time image" which some people may have for any business operating out of a home and still benefit from a low-cost home operation. You can use a Post Office box address if your business is mail order, as Ed B. and many other successful operators do. You can rent a desk in an office building, which will entitle you to the use of a downtown address, as Lloyd H., a manufacturer's representative, does. If you don't have someone around the house all the time to answer the phone, you can tie your phone into an answering service and give the illusion of having a hired secretary as Bill S., the plumber, does. Make arrangements with your answering service to convey the impression that the phone is being answered by a private secretary.

Mary H., who lives in a small town that is relatively near to Atlanta, rents a Post Office Box in Atlanta, and hence has the advantage of a big city address. The same idea applies to renting desk space in a building in an adjoining, larger city.

If you're doing mail order business or a business involving a considerable amount of correspondence, you can create a solid image with well-designed, high-quality letterheads and stationery. Attractive brochures will also help to convey the image of bigness and substantiality.

CUT OVERHEAD WITH SERVICES
THAT COST ONLY WHEN WORKING

You can keep your expenses low by minimizing the number of full-time employees that you have in your business. Then the services that these employees would normally perform can be obtained either under contract or on a time-and-materials basis. You pay only for specific services that you receive. If you purchase these services from other businesses, you'll be helping them to pay for the overhead associated with the work that is being done for you. However, you do not have to maintain the full overhead yourself. You can even eliminate paying someone else overhead plus profit by enlisting the services of individuals directly; hence, you pay only the per hour earnings. Typical non full-time services in a small business are typing, printing, janitorial, drafting, engineering design, etc. You can usually effect further savings working with individuals by employing moonlighters who utilize their extra time to make extra money.

Some of the services that you will require will have to be paid on a per job basis. Others will have to be paid on an hourly basis. In cases involving quantity, the work can be let out as "piece work." This includes manufacturing operations (cutting, sewing, painting, plating, etc.), repair service (TV, lawnmowers, air conditioners, etc.), and even office service, such as envelope addressing.

You can reduce selling costs to a "pay-for-results-only" basis by putting your salesmen on commission or selling through a distributor.

The idea of using services that cost only while working is not confined to small businesses. Numerous large businesses pay for services that cost only when working because it would be unprofitable for them to maintain a full-time employee for the amount of work that is involved. Gary George, an accountant, uses Kelly Girls and rents extra calculators during the tax season (December through April). In many instances, the cost of the employee and the cost of capital equipment becomes a consideration. Where capital equipment is involved and the use of the equipment would be minimal, it is desirable to place the work outside on a cost-only-while-working basis. Mabel L.'s interior decorating service has special decorative and furnishing items made in a woodworking shop; she sends items to be painted to a professional painter.

MONEY-SAVING EQUIPMENT IDEAS

There are a number of ways in which you can save money on equipment and consequently have a larger amount of operating capital. One of the ways of doing this has already been cited; namely, to use outside services. Another way to save money on equipment is to rent equipment, such as sanders, waxers, impact drills, etc., that is not required continually. If equipment, such as a lathe, is required on a continuous basis, you may be able to save some money by buying a used one. However, you can sometimes get stuck with used tools and machines that fail after a short period of use or require extensive repair. Be sure that any used tools or machines that you purchase are operating and bear the telltale signs of user pride and care indicative of good maintenance.

A frequent pitfall of new businesses is that the owners become enamoured with gadgetry and equipment; they buy *more* fancy electronic testers than they actually need to do the job. For some requirements, you can obtain multifunctional machines (e.g., a combination saw and joiner) which can do two or more jobs. Use the least expensive and least sophisticated equipment that you can get without suffering considerable employee time losses. Schedule and share equipment in your shop and office. When you discover that a piece of equipment is lying around and not being used, dispose of it and get the cash back into your business.

HOW TO FIND A LOW-COST BUSINESS LOCATION

We've discussed location in an earlier chapter. Here we want to mention some unusual low-cost location opportunities that may present themselves. Manufacturing, service, and other businesses that do not require fronts can sometimes be located in run-down buildings or in run-down parts of town. Typical examples are foundries, plating or painting operations, dress factories, furniture factories, plumbers, electricians, repair men, building contractors, etc. Keep your eye open for empty stores and for run-down houses in areas that have been rezoned commercial, retail, or industrial. Old houses make good antique shops, bargain stores, and small factories. You can sometimes rent these locations for considerably less than you can rent dead warehouse space. If crime and destruction runs high in the area, avoid it. Pay a little more rent for the safety that a better location affords you and your property.

Another source of low-cost business locations is unused space in office and other business buildings. The space may be run-down and fix-up may be uneconomical to the owner for the amount of rent the space would bring. (I started a small woodworking operation in an old equipment room of one of my buildings.) In some cases the space cannot be upgraded. Typical locations of such space are old furnace rooms, attics, and old storage rooms. One of the best ways to uncover this type of space is to talk to the building superintendent.

If you're going into manufacturing, it may be possible for you to locate in a small town on the outskirts of your city. You may find a locality where business is slow and where abandoned stores which can be used as factories are available at low cost. A large ladies' dress factory uses just such a location, twenty miles from downtown Dallas.

Another way to obtain a low-cost factory is to lease a factory that belongs to a community which is anxious to build its labor force. Sometimes communities have these factories ready-built or will build to suit. They'll give you a long-term lease at a very low rate to raise employment in the community.

COST SHARING

It is possible to effect economies in the operation of your business through cost sharing with another business. Here are some of the ways in which you can make this work.

You can sometimes find a business location that is larger than what you need at a very reasonable rent. If you can get another business to share the location with you, you can split the rent and hence both benefit from the rent cost savings. If your businesses are related but non-competitive, you may be able to share the telephone and effect further savings. A plumber and an air conditioning serviceman could capitalize on this. If both of the businesses are retail, the two businesses might jointly hire one individual to tend both stores. For example, a real estate man and an insurance man can share the same secretary.

You can effect savings through cost sharing on equipment. For example, if both businesses require a delivery truck but the demand is not sufficiently great to require two trucks, share the delivery truck and cut delivery expenses in half. The same applies to expensive machinery. The possibilities are infinite if you're willing to take the time and effort to develop them.

RENT, BUY, OR BUILD?

The decision to rent, buy, or build is usually an easy one

for the starting business. Here are the pros and cons of each of these approaches.

Renting requires only a very small initial outlay of cash. However, you're helping the landlord to pay for the building. On the other hand, you may be able to rent for less than you could possibly buy or build since the building may have been built a number of years ago, when building costs were considerably lower. If you rent, the lease with renewal options will give you a high degree of permanency. However, a lease obligates you for the full term and amount of the lease. It involves a sizeable obligation.

You may be able to buy a building for your business with a relatively small cash down payment and with monthly payments that are considerably less than the rent that you'd have to pay. In this case, the initial cash outlay would probably be higher than the initial cash outlay if you were renting; however, you'll save the landlord's profit each month. If you can buy a building that is larger than what you need for your requirements, you may be able to sublet enough space in the building to get your space rent free.

If you already own land that is properly zoned, you might want to consider building. If the value of the land is great, you may be able to build and obtain financing that doesn't involve any additional outlay of assets (other than the lot) on your part. To explore the situation, develop a rough sketch of the building that you would have built. Then get several tentative bids on the cost of constructing the building. Next, see a savings and loan or mortgage company to determine how much you can borrow for constructing the building and the terms under which you can get the financing. For example, if your lot is worth $20,000 and you want to put up an $80,000 building, if you can obtain an 80 per cent loan ($80,000), you won't have to invest a cent if you own the lot free and clear. (Generally speaking, your best bet is renting or buying when you're starting a business. You

would generally build only if you had very special requirements that couldn't be met through the rental or the purchase of an existing building.)

TWENTY-EIGHT WAYS
TO CUT EXPENSES

Business profit is a function of sales, cost of goods, and
expenses. If you can cut expenses, you can increase your
business profits. We've cited some ways in which you can
cut expenses earlier; here are some more. First use these
eight specific ways to control purchasing and selling costs:

1. When you buy, shop or take bids.
2. Buy used equipment whenever possible.
3. Check your office and janitorial supplies periodically to determine whether you're overstocking.
   Work down overstock and eliminate purchasing
   till levels are substantially reduced.
4. Avoid inventory stockpiling. Interest costs and
   possible obsolescence are expensive.
5. Purchase in quantity to get better prices.
6. Use charge accounts to minimize money costs.
7. Take discounts (2 per cent/ten days is more than
   70 per cent simple interest!)
8. Watch for auctions, closeouts, and liquidations.

Production and operating costs can be reduced by following these ten rules:

1. Minimize equipment costs by making equipment
   work harder and longer.
2. Minimize employee costs by doing as much of it
   yourself as you can.
3. Employ preventative maintenance to avoid expensive equipment repair bills.
4. Employ a simplified bookkeeping system.
5. Organize service and production facilities for maximum efficiency.

6. Keep your employees by maintaining a tolerant and pleasant working atmosphere. It's expensive to train new employees.
7. Avoid organizational frills. Minimize the number of executives and specialized departments that you set up in your business.
8. If you're in manufacturing or service, study the service or production techniques in use and improve them whenever possible.
9. Maintain maximum comfort in working areas. Minimize comfort in "goof-off" areas such as rest rooms and lounges.
10. Keep accurate accounts of your various costs in order to exercise maximum control.

Here are ten guidelines for reducing administrative, general and miscellaneous overhead costs:

1. Avoid frills that add little to your profit possibilities.
2. Minimize communication costs by using informal hand-written memos.
3. Avoid bank service fees by keeping your checking account balances above the minimum.
4. Use standard billing and other business forms to minimize printing costs.
5. Minimize filing costs by filing only important papers.
6. Clean your files out periodically to avoid excessive storage cabinet costs and to increase operating efficiency.
7. Reduce utility costs by turning off lights, air conditioning or heat, and other utility-consuming appliances at night and over the weekend.
8. Minimize telephone costs by using special time rates.
9. Reduce long distance costs through telephone appointments that enable you to call station-to-station rather than person-to-person.
10. Group your sales calls geographically to minimize travel expense and time.

HOW TO REDUCE MAINTENANCE COSTS

Reduce maintenance costs on your property by conducting a regular preventative maintenance program. Touch up the paint frequently to avoid total repainting. Clean furnaces, air conditioners, and other appliances to avoid expensive breakdowns. Always keep extra floor tiles and carpet remnants so that you can make repairs without redoing the entire job.

If you have rental properties, you can cut maintenance costs by minimizing the services that you provide. For example, if rentals are low, you can have your tenants accept that you will skip or reduce janitorial service, supplying paper goods for rest rooms, not furnish utilities, or service air conditioning, heating, and lighting equipment, and other side activities sometimes incidental to rental. If you do this, insist on the right to inspect your property and require the tenant to conduct preventative maintenance on your equipment on a regular basis. If you do furnish these services, be sure that you have an adequate pad over and above the net lease price to be able to furnish them at a profit.

HOW TO PROFIT ON FIFTY YEARS' EXPERIENCE IN TWO HOURS

An extremely important tactic that will save money and maximize your profit is the maximum utilization of your ears and your eyes. Use your eyes to study books and periodicals which deal with business, particularly with the business in which you are engaged. Use your ears to benefit from the experience of other businessmen. Visit other businessmen and discuss methods of operation with them. Most businessmen are proud of the way they operate and will gladly share their experiences with you. Hence, you can get many years' experience in an hour or two.

There are a number of inexpensive business publications

that deal with specific businesses that are available to you. Take advantage of these, too.

WHERE TO GET INEXPENSIVE PUBLICATIONS ON SPECIFIC BUSINESSES

You have access to a substantial quantity of business literature through your public library, the Small Business Administration, and other sources. You'll find a large number of books and special manuals in the public library that deal with a broad array of businesses in very specific terms. In addition to these books which you can borrow and use, there are books that are available through the U.S. Government at very low cost. These books include technical manuals prepared for the military services, as well as publications of the Small Business Administration.

The starting and managing series published by the Small Business Administration (SBA) includes books on a number of businesses. The "Starting and Managing Series" includes:

"Starting and Managing a Small Credit Bureau and Collection Service."

"Starting and Managing a Service Station."

"Starting and Managing a Bookkeeping Service."

"Starting and Managing a Building Business."

"Starting and Managing an Aviation Fixed Base Operation."

"Starting and Managing a Motel."

"Starting and Managing a Duplication and Mailing Service."

"Starting and Managing a Restaurant."

"Starting and Managing a Retail Hardware Store."

"Starting and Managing a Retail Drug Store."

"Starting and Managing a Dry Cleaning Business."

"Starting and Managing an Automatic Vending Business."

"Starting and Managing a Car Wash."

"Starting and Managing a Swap Shop or Consignment Sales Shop."

"Starting and Managing a Small Shoe Service Shop."

These publications can be ordered from the Superintendent of Documents, Government Printing Office, Washington, D. C. 20402. The cost ranges from about 25 cents to a dollar each.

SMALL BUSINESS ADMINISTRATION SERVICES

Small Business Administration has an additional broad array of publications which are available through the U.S. Government Printing Office. It will be worth your while to contact your local U. S. Department of Commerce Office. They have lists of available publications and generally stock them for direct purchase. If there's no field office near you, you can get ordering information from the Superintendent of Documents.

The Small Business Administration also conducts an advisory service. You can visit your local Small Business Administration office and discuss your business problems with SBA representatives. In addition, SBA conducts local classes from time to time that may prove valuable.

WHAT YOUR ACCOUNTANT CAN DO FOR YOU

Engage the service of an accountant to assist you in setting up your books and to advise you on tax matters. You may wish to use him to perform all of your bookkeeping rather than use an employee. Your accountant can spot places where you can increase efficiency, eliminate expenses, get tax breaks, and otherwise improve your profit picture. An accountant usually has a good knowledge of businesses, since he services numerous clients. He can save you hundreds and even thousands of dollars in expenses, taxes, and other costs.

WHAT YOUR BANKER CAN TEACH YOU

Your banker can teach you quite a bit about business. He has seen businesses rise and fall over the years, has provided financing for them, and has maintained contact with business problems. It's always a good idea to seek the advice of your banker when you're contemplating substantially large steps in your business. Your banker can advise you on finance, can tell you of some of the pitfalls others have run into with similar plans before you, and he may know of a pertinent current event or activity that might affect what you're contemplating. The banker generally knows what's going on in the business community and can also serve as a source of information as well as a source of knowledge.

OTHER SOURCES OF BUSINESS
COUNSEL AND INFORMATION

You can obtain business counsel from a wide variety of sources. Your *Chamber of Commerce* can give you business information and, in some instances, counsel. *Insurance agents* can advise you on insurance matters; *real estate people* can advise you on real estate matters. If you're contemplating the purchase or installation of mechanical equipment, the *manu-facturer's representatives* can provide competent counsel. By counselling with several of them, you will get a multi-sided view of the pros and cons to help you arrive at wise decisions. The businessman who uses his eyes and his ears to take advantage of the experience of others will generally out-prosper the businessman who plunges doggedly ahead with his eyes and ears closed.

Chapter 10

A $2,000 START MAKES YOU A
WHEELER-DEALER

MERLIN K. BECOMES A
WHEELER-DEALER

A $2,000 start (or your first $2,000 profit) can set you up as a wheeler-dealer.

Merlin K. started a shoe repair business with $50. His business prospered. After a year of operation, he had an extra nest egg of $2,000 that wasn't required for the operation and further growth of his shoe repair business. He scanned the "Business Opportunity" want ads searching for a new venture. He liked this one:

> For Sale — Italian restaurant. Same location ten years.
> Short hours — 10 A.M. — 6 P.M.
> Nets $30,000. Phone

It was the "Nets $30,000" that caught his eye and sparked his interest. He called and learned that the asking price for the business was $60,000, with 25 per cent down payment required. This was out of his league, but he decided to investigate anyway. He visited the restaurant as a customer. It was neat and well run, and the food was good. He learned from the waitress that the owner did the cooking and that he was elderly. This confirmed Merlin's estimate of the owner from the telephone conversation.

Merlin decided to investigate further. He asked to see the owner and was given a tour of the kitchen. Then he asked to see the books. He found that the owner's salary made up part of the stated net. The additional salaries required to do the work the owner was doing himself still left the net around $20,000. When he looked into the lease, he found it had four years to go with a five-year renewal option. So far, so good.

Merlin told the owner that he was interested, but that the price was too stiff.

"Make an offer," the owner said.

Merlin offered $30,000 verbally. The owner gave him a hard, disgusted no. Merlin left. Two days later Merlin presented a written contract offering $35,000 plus a food inventory cost with $4,000 cash down. The owner folded the contract, stuck it in his pocket and said he'd think about it. The owner called that evening and said he'd take $37,000 plus inventory cost with $5,000 down. Merlin decided to take the deal. He borrowed $4,000 on a signature loan which, with his $2,000 nest egg, gave him $6,000, enough to handle the down payment, handle rent proration, and put some operating cash in the till. The contract stipulated that the previous owner would stay on for two weeks without pay till Merlin took hold. Merlin hired a cook, advertised the restaurant more effectively, promoted the hostess to manager, put the waitresses into attractive uniforms, and increased business 25 per cent in a month. He paid off the $4,000 he had borrowed on his signature in three months, and netted a true $35,000 the first year! That left him with plenty of spendable (investable!) cash, since he had a three-year payout on the restaurant. He put this spendable cash into stocks and real estate, and began to wheel and deal in earnest.

NEW BIG DOLLAR PROFITS ARE YOURS

After you've earned your first $2,000 in cash profit, you're ready to take on bigger and better ventures that have tremendous profit opportunities, just as Merlin did. You're in a good position to enter the areas of construction, finance, investment, and real estate rentals. In this chapter, you'll learn how to wheel and deal in big profits with modest amounts of your own cash.

MAKE SIZEABLE PROFITS IN CONSTRUCTION

Profits in construction are big because the size of the sale is generally large. The aggressive builder can also achieve sizeable volume in his business. The ease with which improved property can be financed, the rapid growth in population, and the demand for homes, offices, retail buildings, and government buildings to service this growing population build vast profit possibilities.

A building is generally erected on a contract basis. Ed B., a prime contractor (builder), breaks the job up into a number of subcontract jobs. Thus, as the builder, he is simply a manager, with no actual construction capability of his own. Some builders have construction capability in one or more of the areas that Ed lets out on subcontract.

Ed uses a foundation contractor, a framing contractor, a brick contractor, a roofing contractor, an electrical contractor, a plumbing contractor, a mechanical (air conditioning and heating) contractor, etc. At the outset of the project, he obtains plans for the house or the building to be erected. He solicits bids for each of the subcontract areas. He takes the most favorable bids and uses these subcontractors to bid and do the job.

Joe G. is a home builder. He builds houses for sale. He may build the houses to the specifications of the purchaser, or he may build the houses and then look for purchasers afterward. When he does this, the house is called a spec (speculation) house. He must purchase building lots to operate. He generally manages this by getting options on the land and getting a loan commitment for the finished houses. He obtains an interim loan commitment, which provides short-term money during construction. When he finds a buyer, he knows how much a qualified buyer is going to be able to borrow on the house. The buyer fills in a credit questionnaire, and if the financing institution accepts the buyer, the loan commitment on a house changes from a tentative to a firm loan commitment.

Joe G. uses his interim money as he proceeds with construction on the property. Sometimes his arrangements permit him to get interim money from the bank as he needs it to pay off subcontractors rather than taking a lump sum of money which will be idle during most of the construction process. When he completes construction and has gone through the various inspections, he arranges for a closing on the property. When the property is closed and the mortgage is placed, the buyer is on the note for the long-term payout on the property, and Joe gets the money to pay the interim off and take his profit. Joe makes $1,000 to $3,000 on each house that he builds. He has invested less than $1,000 in his business.

In soliciting subcontracts, Joe usually obtains three to five bids for each portion of the task. In his subcontracts, he specifies the period of time for performance. In some instances, he incorporates penalty clauses for schedule slippage into the subcontracts. Time is an important factor in the cost of construction because delays are costly, subcontractor interface problems may arise, and the interest on the interim money continues to run till the house is sold. Some small town builders utilize moonlighters on their jobs. This is particularly true with interior work that can be done after regular working hours or during bad weather. In larger towns labor unions, codes, and local situations may preclude the use of moonlighters.

The general building contractor who builds to a specification for a customer does not speculate. When a new building is to be erected, a bid package is submitted to contractors who are interested. The contractor studies the plans and gets tentative bids from his subcontractors. He puts the whole bid together and submits it. A bid opening (formal or informal) takes place and the contract is awarded.

There's quite a bit of profit in the remodeling and small add-on building business. It's so good that Hap L. quit real estate sales altogether to go full-time in remodeling. This work is much smaller scale than larger construction projects and it's easier to utilize part-time help for small jobs. Furthermore, the jobs are easier to sell and you spend less time trying to sell an individual job. These jobs usually range from $500 to $5,000 in total value. To get this type of business, place a small classified ad under the "Services" or "Building"Classified section of your newspaper.

Another possibility in the construction business is to construct your own buildings for rental purposes. That's the subject of the next section, "The Secrets of Buy-Rent." In this section you'll learn how to earn a perpetual income through rentals. You can pyramid your profits by buying land, developing it yourself, and then renting the structures that you erect on it.

THE SECRETS OF BUY-RENT

Buy and rent to make big profits. In the rental business you never give up your product and you derive continual income from it. Furthermore, you can finance the majority of your purchases by using the purchased object (which you are going to rent) as collateral. Another advantage to the rental business is that you can depreciate the purchased object and hence gain a tax advantage.

The traditional big ticket rental involves real estate. My rental properties return 10 per cent to 40 per cent annually on investment. During the last century, numerous other items have gone into the rental catalog. These include factory equipment, automotive equipment, tools, sick room appliances, and household items, to mention only a few.

To get an idea how the rental business operates, let's assume that you enter the general rental business, renting tools and household appliances as Dan W. did. He purchased a floor buffer for $100. He paid $10 down and financed the balance. He rents the buffer for $2 a day. He can rent the buffer ten days a month and realize an income of $20 a month from the rental. He financed the buffer for a period of eighteen months, with payments of $5 a month, and an interest charge of 1 per cent of the unpaid balance. His first payment was $5.00 plus $.85 (1 per cent of the unpaid balance of $85.). Hence, he had a cash flow of $14.15, and in addition paid off $5 of the principal during the first month. His first month's net profit was $19.15. Notice that his net was more than his initial investment of $10 during the first month. From time to time the buffer will require maintenance. Even so, he's still making a healthy profit.

Buy-rent activities are top moneymakers. The investment requirements are low since the rented property provides loan collateral, and the renters make the loan payments and provide additional spendable profits.*

TAP REAL ESTATE CAPITAL GAINS

Tap real estate capital gains. Real estate tends to go up in value with time. Hence, if you buy a property and hold it from three to five years, you can generally sell it at 1-1/2 to 3 times what you paid for it. This produces a sizeable profit, even if it were taxed as ordinary income. However,

---

Successful Moonlighting Techniques That Can Make You Rich by Forrest H. Frantz, Sr. (Parker Publishing Co.) treats rent-lease techniques in detail.

under the tax laws in existence at the time this book was written, you are entitled to pay the capital gains tax on any property that you have held for more than a year. Your capital gains tax is computed at a lower rate than ordinary income tax. Thus, you have a higher percentage of spendable income over and above what you have with ordinary income profit.

Another advantage that makes real estate capital gains investments attractive is the property collateral feature. Thus, you purchase a property for as little as 5 per cent, 10 per cent, or 20 per cent down. Your out-of-pocket investment is small in proportion to the gain. The interest that you pay on the balance is tax deductible.

FORM AND PROFIT FROM SYNDICATES

If a business or property investment requirement exceeds your own capabilities, you can form a syndicate with other investors and pool your investment capability. The syndicate may take the form of a partnership or a corporation. Each of the investors shares in the profits according to the percentage of his part of the total investment. If you have ten partners in the syndicate and each puts up $1,000, each owns 10 per cent of the total investment. Syndicates are commonly used in the real estate field, but can be applied to other business ventures as well.

You can own an equity in a syndicate without actually putting up the cash. Here's the way big operators do it.

Suppose you find the deal and then interest nine other investors in putting in $1,000 each. In return for finding and promoting the deal, you get your 10 per cent share of the action free. Although only $9,000 in cash was put into the venture, you put in $1,000 worth of effort, making the full value worth $10,000. Realtors frequently put syndicates together and earn a commission from the property seller in addition to earning participation in the syndicate.

EARN BIG RETURNS

Make investments that will earn big returns. You're in a better position to do this as your available cash and credit reputation grows. Two thousand dollars or more is a substantial amount of cash to wave in front of a prospective seller. This gives you an advantage in the purchase of real estate, businesses, and equities in businesses. With $2,000 cash, you stand a good chance of buying a property worth as much as $50,000. Here's how I've done it. The $2,000 cash position and increased net worth placed me in a position to borrow $5,000 on a signature loan. This gave me $7,000 to use as a down payment. The balance of $43,000 was debt secured by a mortgage on the property. When there's a mortgage on the property already, try to assume the mortgage and give the seller a second for the balance. You can often get into a $50,000 deal with a $2,000 down payment when these conditions prevail.

PICK PROFITABLE EQUITY INVESTMENTS

With $2,000 in cash, you can buy a profitable equity in a business. In some instances, $2,000 will make a down payment or purchase 100 per cent of a business. You'll recall that Merlin K. started with $2,000 of his own money, pyramided it, and got a business originally priced at $60,000.

When you're looking at a business as a possible purchase, determine why the owner desires to sell. There are a number of things that may cause him to sell for considerably less than he is asking for the business. These things include:

1. Consistent losses (The owner gets anxious to sell at any price.)
2. A need for cash (A note which could wipe the owner out falls due soon. He'll sell cheap to avoid foreclosure.)
3. Ill health (Owner needs "out" to care for his health. He'll sell cheap if he has to.)

4. Desire to enter other employment or another business (Owner is fed up with the business, although it's profitable. He wants to try something else.)
5. Personal conditions, which may require a move or which may involve his personal situation. (Divorce, wanting to be close to his children, or wanting to move to another part of the country.)
6. Legal problems (Owner must settle judgment or leave state to avoid suit.)
7. Any of other numerous reasons.

Check inventory, equipment, and the lease on his property, just as Merlin K. did. Watch the place of business from time to time for several days to determine the volume of business. Ask to examine books and compare what the books tell with what you observed in surveying his business. If you study the business adequately, you'll avoid a bad buy and save yourself headaches in the future. When you make an offer, always offer less than what's asked.

LEND MONEY FOR PROFIT

You can't expect to realize the return from lending operations that you can achieve with equity investments. However, as you continue to prosper and accumulate wealth, you'll want to diversify your investments. First lien notes on residential and business property are attractive because they offer good security. They also offer reasonable interest and an additional bonus at the time the loan is made in the form of points for making the loan. Here's a typical deal. A man needing $2,000 went to Len J. for a loan. Len knew the man was a good worker — steady and honest. His house was clear, so Len was well protected when he gave him a $2,000 loan on his $15,000 house and took a mortgage on it. He lent the money at 10 per cent interest. (You can sometimes obtain a one or two point fee in addition. Hence, you might lend $2,000, minus 2 per cent, or a total of $1,960 for his $2,000 note.) You would collect 10 per cent interest or $200 during the first year if the loan is a balloon loan (total principal due at some time in the future). It's wiser to get monthly interest payments where you collect the interest faster and can start putting some of it to work in a month.

HOW TO MAKE GOOD DEALS COME YOUR WAY

You can make good business deals come your way by letting people know that you're looking for them. Here are some of the ways in which you can let people know that you're looking for deals:

1. Advertisements in the classified "Opportunities Wanted" section
2. Word-of-mouth
3. Telephone calls
4. Contact with lawyers, realtors, and business brokers
5. Discussions with bankers

As your reputation as a businessman and entrepreneur grows, you will have more good and bad deals presented to you than you can possibly handle. I have had as many as twenty propositions presented to me during a single week. Unfortunately, you'll receive a lot of bad or marginal propositions along with the good. Consequently, you can spend an awful lot of time listening. In due time you learn how to handle them and minimize time wasted in listening to bad or marginal deals.

USE FINANCIAL SKILL TO INCREASE MARGINS

Use financial skill to increase your margins of profit. You can increase your profits by increasing resale price, by cutting overhead, by mechanizing, and by decreasing the cost of money. Review Chapters Six and Nine. Master these fund raising, expense cutting, and wise buying strategies to increase your volume of business action and the size of your profits.

SURE DEALS IN THE STOCK MARKET

From time to time there are sure deals in the stock market. One type of deal that always involves a sure profit is an *arbitrage* situation. An arbitrage situation exists when you can purchase and sell the same securities, commodities, or foreign exchange simultaneously in different markets at a profit due to unequal prices. Assume, for example, that two corporations are to merge. The stock of one corporation is valued at $14, and the stock of the other corporation is valued at $11. Assuming that the stockholders of the 14 point stock were to receive 1.4 shares of the 11 point stock for each stock held, it becomes apparent that you can profit by buying the 14 point stock and selling the 11 point stock. Here's how it works.

Value of 1 share $11 stock $= 11 \times 1.4 = 15.4$
Value of 1 share $14 stock $\qquad = 14.0$
Gross profit/share $\qquad\qquad 1.4$

You buy the 14 point stock long and sell the 11 point stock short. Your profit will be reduced by the amount of the brokerage fees, but the profit is still a reasonable one. Tentative mergers usually create arbitrage situations.

Another sure profit deal exists in the market when a corporation is to be liquidated and the assets have a book value in excess of the stock selling price. In this case, you can profit by buying the stock which might be selling for 10 points while the liquidation will produce $14 per share. You would have a profit of some 40 per cent on your investment.

Most of the activity in the stock market is based on day to day trading of stocks; of buying stocks at low prices, holding them for an increase, then selling them, or in a declining market, selling the stocks short and then covering the stock when the price falls. Day to day trading in the stock market requires considerable experience and expertise. Although a few amateurs have done well in the market, most stock market investors suffer losses till they gain enough experience to know how to invest and trade profitably.

HOW TO GAIN EXPERTISE IN THE STOCK MARKET

If you re going to invest in the stock market, you'd better invest from a base of knowledge and experience. You can get plenty of tips from investors, brokers, and others. These so-called tips sometimes are useful, but more often than not can lead you to losses. If you're going to invest in the stock market, I recommend that you study a number of books on the subject. After you've gotten the general flavor of the stock market, start to follow the market daily in the *Wall Street Journal*. Pick several stocks and go through the paper exercise of investing imaginary money. Allot yourself an amount of money, say $10,000, then pick the stocks that you would buy. Watch them for several days and decide when you'll sell. This paper experience doesn't cost a penny since you haven't actually bought the stocks, yet it will teach you quite a bit about the stock market.

In addition to study and paper practice, I recommend some visits to a stock brokerage office. Watch the activity on the boards. You can also learn quite a bit by talking to traders who gather in the stock broker's offices. Many of them make a living by playing the stock market.

KEEP EMOTION OUT OF BIG DEALS

Save yourself money and make bigger future profits by keeping emotion out of your deals. Don't buy a building or a property because it catches your fancy or because you find it exciting. Don't buy a stock because the name sounds exciting or for some other reason not founded on experience and logic. Don't buy a business because it appears to be a prestige business, but only if you can see a logical profit potential in the deal.

The matter of keeping emotion out of the deal applies to selling as well as buying. Don't sell a property because it suddenly has a lot of headaches connected to it. Cure the headaches first, then sell the property. If you do this, you'll sell the property at a greater dollar value.

KEEP YOUR MONEY TURNING

As you start to receive income from your investments, put the money to work in other new ventures. As you sell merchandise off your shelves, replace the merchandise and add new lines. Keep your money turning perpetually and rapidly in order to achieve the highest possible earnings. A $1,000 inventory turned twenty times a year is more profitable than a $10,000 inventory turned once a year.

EYEBALL THE FUTURE

Eyeball the future to detect trends and events that can create situations for profit. Rising employment, increasing interest rates and increasing sales are signs of an expanding economy. If you see good times ahead, invest heavily. Rising unemployment, decreasing interest rates and decreasing sales signal a recession. If you see bad times ahead, pull in your horns. Keep an eye on technology. Watch newspapers, the Wall Street Journal, and scientific publications. Get in on the ground floor on new technological advances to profit on the future. I did this back in 1953 by designing transistorized devices when the transistor was in its infancy.

Mike L. foresaw a housing shortage in 1966. He started to buy houses. He rented the houses, and then in 1969 and

1970, when housing was scarce, he sold them. An initial investment of $5,000 made a total of $40,000 for him — $30,000 of this was in capital gains.

Frank S. became concerned with the pollution situation in 1967. He started to develop an electronic precipitator in his garage. In 1970, he went into the market with his precipitator. Sales have been good and his business is growing rapidly.

Andy S. foresaw boom years ahead in 1964. He bought a number of fast food franchises, and today his original investment of $15,000 is worth three-quarters of a million dollars.

GET AND USE INSIDE INFORMATION

There's an undercurrent of discussion and information in the business world that is useful to the investor and the entrepreneur. These channels of discussion and inside information include bankers, real estate brokers, insurance people, government employees, lawyers, and leaders in the community. While most of this information is not held as top secret, it is nevertheless quietly and discreetly conveyed. You can only fall heir to this information by functioning in civic organizations and by maintaining your contacts with these people in your community. As they accept you and begin to respect your accomplishments, you'll find that they'll open doors to information that was never before available to you. Much of this information will be useful in making your investments and in operating your businesses.

Chapter 11

GET RICH IN SPITE OF
ADVERSITY, HARD TIMES,
AND FIERCE COMPETITION

WHY OPPORTUNITIES ARE GREATER
WHEN TIMES ARE BAD

The air conditioning, automotive, and radio industries grew into their own during one of the fiercest depressions that ever hit the United States. Many of the top 100 U. S. industries were born or underwent early growth during periods of recession. Bad times are a two-way street. Although it's a little harder for the businessman to sell, he has the advantage of lower cost supplies, materials, and labor. Furthermore, he has opportunities to buy and invest at prices that enable him to make tremendous profits. Recession and depression test the resourcefulness of a businessman. Anyone can make money during booming times, but the resourceful businessman can be outstandingly successful even in bad times.

When times are bad, people become pessimistic. They

think the times will get even worse. Many give up, many are frustrated, and many decide to ride along with reduced earnings and reduced living standards.

You, as a go-getter businessman, say "No" to all of this. You invest during hard times; consequently you can buy equity positions, whole businesses, and property for considerably less than you can in good times. Money is cheaper, labor and material costs are less, so you invest during hard times. By judiciously managing your enterprises, you make them service debts that you incurred in acquiring them. Then, as times improve, your already established and working business bases begin to earn bigger profits. Your investment is smaller than it would have been if you bought during good times. Your percentage return on investment oftentimes reaches several thousand per cent. This places you in a position to expand your business empire faster and allows you to grasp new, bigger, additional business opportunities.

Some businesses do more business during a recession than they do in good times. *The service businesses generally are better during times of recession.* People make things last longer and repair rather than replace. *Any business activity that involves repair and prolonging of life of an object prospers in bad times.*

Bargain stores and cut-rate stores also flourish during recessions and depressions. These include Army-Navy stores, surplus stores, cut-rate drug stores, and second-hand stores. *Stores that provide do-it-yourself tools and do-it-yourself materials prosper in hard times.* These include hardware stores, lumber yards, automobile parts houses, and home gardening equipment and seed centers. Credit collection agencies have increased business during times of recession, too.

Here are some of the kinds of property that can be bought at bargain prices during recessions and depressions:

    1. Raw land

2. Improved property
3. Homes
4. Business and commercial buildings
5. Shop equipment and machinery
6. Store fixtures
7. Luxury items such as boats
8. Jewelry
9. Retail inventories

WAYS TO INCREASE NET WORTH IN BAD TIMES

Bad times offer golden opportunities for increasing net worth. *During bad times you can find bargains* of all sorts, as we've noted in the previous section. Furthermore, *you can usually buy on your own terms.* Thus you not only benefit from a bargain purchase, but you can benefit from better leverage and easier debt financing. Oftentimes you can make side deals that add value to the basic deal. Here are some examples:

Jack W. responded to a classified advertisement offering a drug store for sale. He contacted the owner and went out to look at the drug store. The owner was asking $50,000 for the store. The store cost inventory was $50,000, and he would have gotten the fixtures and the good will of the store free. However, he decided to submit an offer of $30,000 for the store, offering to pay $5,000 down and the balance over a five-year period. The drug store owner rejected the offer but indicated that he would go down to $45,000 and take $10,000 in cash. Jack persisted on a $5,000 payment and eventually ended up getting the business for $38,000. He moved into the business, ran a sale of slow-moving items, and pulled enough cash to pay off the $5,000 in seed money that he had borrowed. Hence, in a matter of a few weeks he owed only $33,000 on the drug store and had a thriving business. The value of the remaining inventory plus the fixtures was equal to roughly twice what he had paid for the business.

Marion B. was acquiring houses. Due to the layoffs in his community, many houses were being signed over simply to anyone who would assume the debt on the houses. He acquired a stable of some twenty houses with a total outlay of only $3,300 cash. He had some vacancies, but was able to rent enough of the houses for them to service the debt on the whole batch. When times began to boom again, he raised his rent, filled his houses, and reaped profits of $4,000 a month.

These are just two examples of how men have increased their net worth in bad times. In the first case, there was an increase in net worth on the order of $30,000 to $40,000, plus the good will of the business. In the second case, the buyer of houses increased his net worth anywhere from $2,000 to $10,000 each time that he assumed a loan on a house. (And, I might add, he can probably refinance them in good times and pull a substantial amount of tax-free cash for new investments!)

HOW TO OUTSELL COMPETITORS IN BAD TIMES

To prosper in hard times you've got to sell more than your competitors. Give your customers these benefits to help yourself sell more:

1. Better quality
2 Better service
3. Guarantees
4. Premiums
5. Delivery service
6. Liberal credit (to qualified purchasers)
7. Variety
8. Price leaders

You may not outsell your competitors by publicizing and providing one or more of these features, but you'll certainly compete. Advertise in your newspaper; put signs in your window; distribute circulars; run direct mail campaigns; use movie, radio, and TV advertising; get the word out and get the customers in. The promotion, advertising, and sales techniques of Chapter Eight deserve extra emphasis in bad times and fiercely competitive situations.

Many businesses cut advertising in hard times. This is the wrong place to cut. Cut your expenses, but do it in other areas than advertising. Remember this: What you spend on advertising is not an indication of the quality of advertising that you are doing. I have seen campaigns that were run on $100 outshine campaigns that cost thousands of dollars. Get yourself right into the middle of it, do a good job with it, and make Chapter Eight pay off for you.

CUT OVERHEAD IN BAD TIMES

You'll always want to be on the alert for opportunities to cut overhead, but you'll especially want to cut overhead during bad times. Put the expense-cutting practices of Chapter Nine to work in a big way. You'll want to be alert to better utilization practices, too.

Shelf space costs money. Think of it as something that has to pay rent. If you have slow-moving items on the shelf, replace them with fast-moving items. You'll be cutting the overhead because you are converting unproductive sales space into productive sales space.

Can you work with fewer employees? Look to your payroll as one possible place to save.

Try to obtain a concession from your landlord. If business is poor and everybody is having a tough time, you might be able to get a 5 per cent to 20 per cent reduction in your rent temporarily. After all, if there's a lot of vacant available space, he'll surely want to see you stay in business in his building.

What about telephones? Are you using two numbers when you might be able to operate your business with just one line? Do you have more extensions that you really need?

Keep expenses down. Cut overhead at all times, but especially in bad times.

TURN ADVERSE CONDITIONS INTO OPPORTUNITIES

Turn adverse conditions into opportunities. All the people who succeed during recessions do so because they turn adverse conditions into opportunity. Most people adopt pessimistic attitudes, and they're the ones who suffer during recessions and depressions. To see the picture in its true perspective, look around you. During periods of recession business is still going on, people are still going to work. The only people who are really in a depression are those who are unemployed. The mass of people react to what they read in print about hard times and respond as though they themselves were having a difficult time. The man who is unemployed during a recession may have been kicked out of the door as far as one particular job goes, but there are still other jobs around. People are getting older and retiring, people are suffering ill health, and some industries are expanding. Consequently, there is always need to replace people leaving industry or to fill new jobs that are being created. This situation prevails during recession as well as during prosperity.

It gets down to this: Most men build what they see about them into extremes — particularly as it applies to reverses. They build these up in their minds until they visualize them as a volcanic eruption about to engulf and bury them. The imagination negatively directed produces a negative outlook. To fight adverse conditions, gain control over your mind. Certainly there'll be reverses; everybody meets them. But in order to turn reverses and adverse conditions into opportunities, you've got to have a quality that I like to call "reboundability." You must be able to bounce back and say, "I'm going to succeed in spite of everything and I'm going to do what I set out to do!" When you meet reverses, turn them around and convert them into opportunity. How do you do it?

First of all, look for constructive elements in the situation. Once, when I submitted an article to a magazine, it came back with a caustic scrawl across the rejection slip that said, "Do you ever read our magazine?" Of course I was incensed. But then as I thought of it, I realized that perhaps what the man was telling me was that if I were to study the magazine I could write an article "to fit" it. I studied the magazine's format and style. A month later I submitted another article and it was accepted. Since then, that magazine has accepted many of my articles.

Another way to use a reversal to an advantage is to treat it as a challenge. A number of years ago I developed an electronic toy. If you're a parent, you may recognize the toy — a calculator with three dials that has been copied many times by many companies. When I first developed this toy calculator I wrote an article about it, and a few months later somebody copied directly from my plans without consulting me. I wrote to the company and got a reply that said in effect, "Yes, we saw your article and put the toy on the market. It's not the talking or writing about it that counts — it's the doing." This toy was not patentable, so I had no legal recourse. I fumed for a few days. Then I got one of their versions of the toy and found that they degraded the product considerably by using cheap parts. So I made an arrangement with another company to market my toy, I enjoyed the moral victory of seeing a better quality product sell at a lower price, and I collected some royalties in the process.

If you're ever tempted to "glum it up" and think of bad times, recession, reverses, and all of that, just consider Columbus. He didn't find his westerly route to the Orient, nor did he discover the intervening American Continent, without trying several times. Helen Keller came into the world with a series of physical reverses — she was deaf, dumb, and blind. These reverses merely served as challenges for accomplishment that few physically sound people realize in their lives. So bounce back. Ignore the negative, dwell on the positive, and work hard to turn adverse conditions into opportunities.

COUNTERATTACK STRATEGY FOR ADVERSITY

Here's some counterattack strategy for adversity. When things look so glum that it seems as if there's no chance to recover at all, pull out a sheet of paper. List the things that you still have in spite of your present state of frustration and/or loss. Do you still have your family? Do you have friends? Do you still have your health? Do you still have your integrity? Do you believe in God and that God stands ready to help you? Okay. After you've jotted down your answers to these questions, think about this for a moment:

Three things determine what happens to you in life. The interim results aren't what count; the total results are what count. First of all, God influences what happens to you. Second, pure chance has something to do with how you make out and what happens to you. Third, but most important, you yourself determine what happens to you! The way *you* take advantage of opportunities that are thrown your way either by the will of God or by chance determines how you make out. It should be apparent that all you need do to prosper in the face of adversity is to get yourself into harness. Decide what you are going to do, how you are going to do it, and then make yourself do it. Don't take no for an answer! Don't falter! Don't step aside at any point along the way! Just go on and do it! Make your profits and re-establish yourself.

HOW TO OVERCOME
FIERCE COMPETITION

When you're in a fiercely competitive situation, your first reaction is to respond to the competitor with like competition. Your emotions tend to rule you, and you can very easily do the wrong thing. Use these three strategies to combat fierce competition:

1. *Respond to a fierce competitive strategy with an unlike strategy of your own.* When Wilson B.'s grocery competitor cut prices, Wilson didn't cut prices to compete with him; he did something else to compete — he started giving trading stamps.

2. *Innovate.* Avoid a "brute force" counterattack. Think about the situation and see what you can do to offer a different enticement to break any competitive lead which his strategy might be scoring for him. For example, when Lloyd's Sewing Center's competitor cut prices on sewing machines, Lloyd counterattacked by stressing guarantees and service in his advertising.

3. *Act on logic — not on emotion.* This will tend to lead you to an innovation that will give you a positive selling advantage over your competitor.

Here are just a few things that you can do to promote your business and overcome fierce competition:

1. *Try a humorous approach in your advertising.* Use a cartoon character to announce the headline on your ad, or use a humorous anecdote or joke in the heading.

2. *Have a bounty hunt.* Steve D. invited his customers to join in the bounty hunt for new customers by way of a letter

to his old ones. He enclosed two introduction cards. His old customers filled in the names of the new prospects plus their own names and addresses. The customers presented the cards to the new prospects and invited them to Steve's Furniture store. The new prospect got a gift (a back scratcher) and a "first sale discount" of 10 per cent. The old customer "bounty hunter" got a $1 gift certificate for each new customer that came in plus a $5 gift certificate if a sale was made. Steve increased his sales $10,000 during the month of the bounty hunt.

3. *Have you checked the sign on the front of your business lately?* Be sure that it's attractive and inviting. Never skimp on sign costs. A cheap sign reflects the image of a cheap, shaky, or amateur business.

4. *Offer a discount or a gift on a package deal.* If you're in the appliance business, you might offer a discount on the combination purchase of a stove and refrigerator.

5. *Use your satisfied customers.* Solicit your customers for permission to print their names with those of other satisfied customers in your ads and in your mailings. This helps to build people's confidence in you.

6. *Watch the newspapers for announcements of new residents, birthdays, and other news about people.* Clip news items about people and send them with a congratulatory note and an invitation to visit your store. You might include a "get acquainted" coupon worth $1. You might send birthday greetings on birthdays and "welcome" letters to new residents.

7. *Sponsor an event.* Sponsor a free amateur show or some sort of contest, or engage a speaker and sponsor the affair in the local meeting hall. The cost is low and the auditorium rental, advertising, and promotion effort will pay off handsomely.

You see, if you use your head you can do a lot more promoting than your competitor is doing.

WHAT TO DO WHEN YOUR COMPETITOR UNDERSELLS YOU

Your fiercest competition from your competitors usually comes in the form of reduced prices. In order to combat this kind of competition, resort to another tactic as we've mentioned earlier. For example, if you employ the bounty hunt or the package discount deal, the satisfied customer idea, or the mailing of newspaper clippings cited in the previous section, you are already effectively combatting a competitor who tries to undersell you.

But never, never get into the price war! There's the old story about the fellow who lost a penny on every banana he sold, but he said, "Look at the business I'm doing!" Don't get caught in this trap.

THE MIND OVER MATTER CONCEPT

By now you should have a pretty good feel for the "mind over matter" concept. It simply means that instead of letting events run you, you take action to run events. The primary idea in the "mind over matter" concept is that of determination. Decide you're going to do it, come hell or high water!

Back up your determination with some faith. It takes a lot of faith to believe that things are going to work out as you planned them, but you can rest assured that if you believe this it is more likely to come to pass than if you don't believe it. A salesman who goes in to sell a customer with the idea that he isn't going to make a sale probably won't, but the one who goes in with the idea that he's going to get the sale usually ends up getting it.

Another factor in the "mind over matter" concept is courage. It takes courage to face some of the things that you encounter in the business world. Courage is defined as the attitude or response of facing and dealing with anything recognized as dangerous or difficult or painful, instead of withdrawing from it. Hemingway defined courage as "grace under pressure." The coward is afraid to tackle a situation that requires courage. Shakespeare wrote, "Cowards die many times before their deaths. The valiant never taste of death but once." It is highly unlikely that you will die in courageously facing a business situation.

Still another factor in the "mind over matter" concept is enthusiasm. Enthusiasm is essential to any success. Your enthusiasm is contagious. Other people are affected by it. If you're enthusiastic, they'll be enthusiastic for your project, your services, and your business. If you're not enthusiastic about it, how in the world do you expect them to be?

HOW I PLUNGED AHEAD IN SPITE OF STAGGERING ODDS

Several years ago, I got very brave and decided to leave a well-paying job with industry to devote full time to my properties. I left my job, got a substantial short-term signature loan, and then plunged ahead to acquire a large property. I leased a portion of the property very quickly, but had to make extensive modifications in the building. During this process, everything in the world seemed to go wrong with every property that I had. A $1,000 air conditioning system for one property, a $700 air conditioning repair bill on another property, several window unit air conditioners breaking down, a lease broken on another property, and the high cost of remodeling the building I had just acquired added up to financial problems.

In spite of all the negatives and a dwindling bank account, I went ahead and tackled the problem segment by segment. It is amazing what you can do with a glut of problems when you divide them into single entities. I did the job, and in a matter of two months had resolved the whole affair into a stable financial situation. So don't let it get you down; tackle it and get it done.

THE ICEBOX TREATMENT

You'll sometimes get into a deal that turns out to be a poor one. It loses money for you and it consumes a disproportionate amount of energy for the returns that it yields. The best bet in this case is to give it the "icebox" treatment.

The "icebox" treatment may take one of several different forms. The first form that it can take is abandonment and storage. If the venture isn't paying off, then simply store all the assets of the business away and forget about them. Concentrate on the aspects of your business that are profitable. At some future date you may either revive or sell the marginal venture.

The second appraoch is to liquidate the assets of the unprofitable business immediately. This gets it into and out of the "icebox" for you. Whenever you're in a situation where you're losing money and the prospects for turning the activity around seem poor, get out or rid of it, and devote your energies to the profitable portion of your business.

WHEN AND HOW TO CHANGE COURSE

The discussion of the "icebox" treatment was not meant to imply that you should divest yourself of any struggling activity or that you should change your direction whenever things go wrong. Any activity that you undertake should be pursued to a reasonable point of profitability or poor potential. Too many people quit too soon. Don't forget that in a horse race, a horse can be last most of the way around the track and still win. Keep this in mind in your business activity, and don't weaken or change course prematurely.

What are some of the signs that it's time to change course? First of all, if the business has been operated for a reasonable amount of time and has not turned profitable, then it may be time to think about changing course — but before you do it, look down the line. Are there any prospects for improvement?

Are there any factors on the economic scene that might change the course of the business? Is the town in which the business located growing? If so, this may be a sign to continue. Are the competitors for this particular business having a difficult time too? If they are, and if one may drop out of business, then those who stay will reap the additional business that he was handling. Is there any federal, state, county or city legislation in process that might affect your business? These and numerous other factors should be considered before you decide to change course. If it still appears doubtful that your business can be turned into a profitable one after you've considered these things, then it's time to change course. In changing course, pick and chart more wisely than you did the first time.

Chapter 12

THE MECHANICS OF
WHEELING AND DEALING

WHEELER-DEALERS MAKE BIG PROFITS

Penny investments can make thousands fast in the wheeler-dealer world! Baxter R. invested about $50, pulled $10,000 tax-free cash in three months, and had a $100,000 property which would pay him about $700 spendable cash a month for ten years (plus pay itself off) and pay him $20,000 a year (and probably more due to appreciation and inflation) thereafter!

Bluntly put, Baxter R. will get $306,000 minimum — probably as much as $500,000 over the next twenty years — on a $50 investment!

$$\frac{\$500,000 \times 100 \text{ per cent}}{\$50} = 1 \text{ million per cent Return!}$$

And when you get right down to it, he didn't really invest

a penny! He took $10,000 tax-free money to launch an enter-
prise that will probably pay him a cool half million dollars
over twenty years — that's an average of $25,000 a year!
Now, prepare yourself to enter a whole new world of quick-
big-BIG-FABULOUS profits. In this chapter you'll learn
about cash-pull financing — Baxter R.'s technique. You'll
discover *short term launching pads* that can catapult you
into the wheeler-dealer world, *debt programming* and *managing for profit,* the *mechanics of making big real estate deals,
how to get unbelievably low interest (below prime!) loans,
how to create and package deals,* and a host of other wheeler-
dealer techniques. In most of the preceeding chapters the
theme was "sure-success." In this chapter, the theme is the
achievement of big-BIG success FAST!

KNOW-HOW ESSENTIAL
TO WHEELER-DEALING

Now, let's get down to the basic secrets and rules of the
wheeler-dealers. These are the rules for making fortunes
with minimum investment (sometimes zero, and sometimes
even pulling pocket cash for assuring yourself profits), fast,
FAST. Chapter Ten showed you how to scratch the surface
once you had a little more cash, but if you're impatient and
have lots of drive, here's how to wheel and deal on a 10 to
100 times greater scope with 1/10 or less as much cash!

Warning! The wheeler-dealer goes after big money fast
with pennies or just a few dollars. He takes big risks —
particularly in terms of losing his "sweat efforts." (But he
usually risks a few or no dollars.) If you're faint-hearted and
would feel defeated after putting in three months of work
without a profit, wheeler-dealing may not be your cup of
tea. But if you're willing to work hard for the big pot of gold
and start over again if you miss it, this chapter is written
especially for you!

The principal "capital equipment" of the big-time wheeler-
dealer is:

1. Know-How
2. Vision
3. Conviction
4. Courage (Guts)
5. Determination

They're all important and essential, but the basis of any deal or course of action is "know-how."

"Know-how" develops from a combination of experience, observation, and study. The starting point is usually study. This book can help you get off the ground. Your public library and your bookstore have plenty of other study materials available. Add to this direct observation of business activities and ventures at the local level, and indirect observation through business and financial publications at the national and international level. Pick up experience by working in someone else's business and then by trying a few things with your own money.

All of this takes a lot of time, but you can greatly reduce the time that it takes if you'll master the fifteen Wheeler-Dealer rules in the next section.

FIFTEEN KEYS TO WHEELER-DEALER SUCCESS

Here's know-how that's made millions:

1. Get paid in advance to make a further profit whenever possible. If you can't —

2. Try to set up your wheeling-deal on a zero or near zero investment.

3. Wheel and deal in any of the ten big profit horizons of Chapter One in which you can make the greatest gain.

4. Capitalize on resources X, Y and Z (Chapter Four) in putting your deal together and selling it.

5. Put the Ten Question Business Selection Test (Chapter Five) to work.

6. Work every possible angle on financing (Chapter Six).

7. Plan your venture to the minutest detail (Chapter Seven).

8. Use the hot sales techniques of Chapter Eight to sell your deal.

9. Sell for the highest possible price.

10. Use "Sweetners" such as credit (small down payment installment plan), side incentives (free radio with a boat, or one drape free with full set of drapes for a house), trades and deferred payments (60 day interest-free charge account), to sell fast and high.

11. Program and manage your cash and debt so that you'll always have cash "in pocket" as well as the means to service debt.

12. Set up alternative plans of action to cope with reverses and contingencies.

13. Know the mechanics of lending, collateralization, and the laws pertaining to equity and debt financing. Make them work for you!

14. To make big bucks fast, make big deals (Jim C. only buys a car for resale when he can make $300 or more on it.)

15. It takes a mammoth creative, mental and physical effort to wheel and deal — but don't ever show it or let anyone know it! Winners always smile!

Those are the guidelines by which the most successful wheeler-dealers make millions; some by adhering to only a few of these guides. Think of what you can do working to all of them!

HOW BAXTER R. FINANCED HIS START

Baxter R.'s fabulous deal worked something like this:

1. He got an option to buy a one acre industrial lot at $20,000. (The owner gave him the option for three months for a $25 consideration because his highest previous offer was $14,000. Baxter didn't know this, but suspected it could be bought for less than $20,000.)

2. He got a buddy who was an engineer and architect to work up preliminary plans for groundwork and a 10,000 square foot building for $25 cash and $1,000 contingent on, and to be paid, upon obtaining financing. (This brought Baxter's investment to $50. Now watch how he put it to work.)

3. Baxter placed ads in several papers under "Business Properties For Rent" and "Industrial Properties For Rent" classifications. He received a number of calls, presented his proposition to several companies, and finally got a ten year lease at $1,670 a month (about $20,000 a year) contingent on his obtaining financing for the building.

4. Simultaneously with step three, Baxter submitted the architect's drawings for the building to three contractors for bids. He received bids of $80,000, $87,500, and $88,600 respectively.

5. He took the lease, the option on the lot, the architect's plans, the three bids, and his financial statement to a mortgage company. He obtained a commitment for a $75,000 dollar loan at 9 per cent with a ten year amortized payout (payments about $950 a month). The loan company arrived at the $75,000 loan by taking 75 per cent of $100,000 ($20,000 for the lot and $80,000 for the building).

6. Next, he went to the owner of the lot and negotiated a contract to buy it at $15,000 — $5,000 below his option!

7. Then, by acting as his own contractor, soliciting bids for the various kinds of work from subcontractors, and figuring on doing the interior painting himself, he found he could cut the building cost to $50,000! Hence his cost would be only $15,000 plus $50,000, or $65,000. Since he borrowed $75,000, he had a pull-out of $10,000 which he could invest in another venture or dispose of as he saw fit. Furthermore, this $10,000 wasn't taxable!

Fabulous? Yes, but it's being done every day in the wheeler-dealer world. This technique (cash-pull financing) is only one of many ways to work a big deal.

SHORT-TERM LAUNCHING PADS

Short-term launching pads are commonly used by shrewd wheeler-dealers to work up to a long-term profit opportunity. Here's how it worked for one wheeler dealer, Tom P.:

1. Tom located a business property consisting of 6,000 square feet of ground with a two story (11,000 square feet) building on it.

2. He made an agreement in principal with the owner to purchase the building for $38,000, with $3,000 cash down.

3. He borrowed $15,000 on a ninety day short-term loan.

4. He bought the building and advertised retail space for rent — "remodeled to suit." (He then had $12,000 of his cash left.)

5. Within thirty days he had signed a lease bringing in $1500 a month. (He got first and last month's rent of $3,000. His cash again was $15,000.)

6. He remodeled the building during the next thirty days at a cost of $13,000. He signed additional tenants for an additional $500 a month, with $1,000 for first and last month's rent. (His cash now was $3,000; his gross monthly income was $2,000.)

That's quite an accomplishment, isn't it? With none of his own money invested, Tom established an annual gross income of $24,000. That's eight times his down payment and 1-1/2 times the remodeling and down payment costs. He'll take in a minimum of $240,000 over the next ten years!

Of course, he was left with a $15,000 note due to his bank within the next thirty days, and he had only $3,000 left. How did he handle this one?

REFINANCE FOR TAX-FREE CASH PULL-OUTS

Our landlord wheeler-dealer who launched his enterprise with a short-term launching pad — a ninety day loan —

solved the payoff dilemma by refinancing. You'll see how it's done by following his subsequent actions:

7. Tom assembled a presentation which included "before" and "after" pictures of the interior and exterior of his building, copies of his leases, his financial statement, and his future plans for the building.

8. He made his presentation to a loan company, asking for a $100,000 loan with a twenty year payout.

9. The loan company had the property appraised and offered to lend $80,000 with a fifteen year payout.

He took the deal. Here's the arithmetic:

Loan		$80,000
Disbursements		
	Payoff original lien	$35,000
	Payoff bank loan	15,000
	1% loan fee	800
	Other closing costs	500
		$51,300
Cash to Wheeler Dealer		$28,700

11. Now Tom, our wheeler-dealer, has $31,700 cash tax-free (that's $28,700 plus the $3,000 he had left), a $24,000 a year gross income, and no short term debt: His monthly payments will be about $820. Insurance, taxes, maintenance, and other expenses will run his total monthly payout to about $1300. His annual *net* cash flow will exceed $8,000, and he has additional net profit in the form of debt amortization!

TRADE ON THE EQUITY

Wheeler-dealers retain full control and full ownership by *trading on the equity*. You trade on the equity when you use your assets to obtain debt financing. The real estate operator does it by securing short- and long-term loans with his real estate holdings. Manufacturers trade on the equity by securing loans with capital equipment as collateral. Corporations trade on the equity by issuing bonds (which are essentially first liens against the business and its assets) and by securing short-term borrowing with specific assets.

There are some interesting aspects to trading on the equity:

1. If a proposition is a sure-fire moneymaker the wheeler-dealer always trades on the equity, because he gets 100 per cent of the profits and has full control.

2. If a proposition is highly speculative, a wheeler-dealer shares the risk by diluting his equity to raise capital. In other words, he incorporates and sells stock. This reduces his percentage of the profits, but it also enables him to avoid debt responsibility.

3. Corporations distribute equity in the form of stock to raise capital. The capital is converted into production assets and provides operating fuel (expense service) for the corporation. When additional funds are needed, the corporation can resort to trading on the equity by issuing bonds and other credit instruments.

4. An interesting result of this series of facts is that you can form a corporation with a small amount of invested capital, and if it is outstandingly successful, you can trade on the equity and hence retain a small, close circle of ownership and control. This has been the basic secret of success of family-owned and controlled corporations.

WHEELER-DEALERS PROGRAM
AND MANAGE DEBT

Wheeler-dealers succeed largely because they understand finance and apply this knowledge to program and manage debt. They borrow short-term money, invest it in assets that can be enhanced in value quickly, conduct the promotion and upgrading that enhances the value, and then use the now valuable asset to obtain long-term financing at the new, larger value. Then they wipe out the short-term debt. Hence they have a long-term moneymaker, cash for new ventures, and short-term borrowing capability for new ventures.

In the process, the short-term borrowing capability of the wheeler-dealer increases. On his first deal, he may only be able to get $2,000. The second time around he can probably get $5,000 to $10,000. And on the third go, he can probably borrow $10,000 to $50,000!

DEBT MECHANICS IN SALE-PURCHASE

The debt mechanisms involved in the sale or purchase of real property, businesses, and equipment are numerous and diverse. You need to understand them to wheel and deal.

A loan is either *secured* or *unsecured.* A seller or lender will generally want his loan secured. However, after you've established a reputation as a businessman and a good credit risk, those with whom you've done business over a long period of time will do business with you on an unsecured basis. The seller or lender's security rests in the fact that your net worth enables him to collect unsecured debt by legal process. In this sense he has security. If you don't have adequate worth, a lawsuit might yield a judgment, but he can't collect money which your assets cannot produce.

Security is usually obtained by a lender or seller within the basic note or by a separate security contract. Mortgages convey a right to title in an asset to the lender or the seller by the borrower or purchaser. When a mortgage is recorded, it becomes a lien. Real estate and chattel mortgages are common mechanisms for securing debt. If the debtor defaults, the lender may foreclose. This destroys the debtor's right to redeem the mortgaged property.

It is possible to mortgage an asset to obtain more than one loan. The first loan is secured by a first mortgage and has precedence over other loans. A second loan secured by the same asset obviously has less strength, since the first lender gets first satisfaction in the event of default.

Here's how to use mortgages to make deals for low cash and big profits:

1. Joe R. needs a forging press for his plant. Henry W., a machine tool broker, has one. The selling price is $50,000. There's an existing loan balance of $30,000 against the machine. Joe has only $5,000 cash.

2. There are several ways for Joe to go:
   (a) Assume the existing debt, give Henry a second mortgage for $15,000, and pay $5,000 cash.
   (b) Obtain a new first loan for $45,000 and pay Henry $5,000 cash.
   (c) If the new first lender will only lend $40,000, give Henry a $5,000 second and $5,000 cash.

3. If the existing first lien has an attractively low interest rate (say 5 1/2 per cent in the face of a 9 per cent current market), give Henry an inducement (e.g., offer an extra $2,000 on the purchase price) to assume the first with a second for the balance.

4. If the existing lien has a short payout, new financing — (b) or (c) above — on a longer term payout might be in order.

When you're selling, the ability to extend credit may mean the difference between "sale" and "no sale." If you can't extend it yourself, help the buyer obtain financing — *but never co-sign his note!*

HOW TO GET INTEREST BELOW PRIME

When you're buying, you can get interest rates below prime rates in special circumstances. If a seller wants to move a property badly enough, he may go below "prime" on the unpaid balance to make the deal. An inducement that you can offer the seller to get a lower interest rate is a larger down payment. I've obtained 5 per cent loans in the face of an 8 1/2 per cent prime (9 1/2 per cent commercial) loan market. That represents a savings of $450/year on each $10,000 on the note, or $4,500/year on a $100,000 loan!

There's another angle to play for low interest. If the seller is in a capital gains position, offer a slightly higher price to get a lower interest rate. He saves on taxes. You save on overall cost and have the advantage of a higher cost basis on your depreciation, and hence lower tax costs.

"PIECE OF THE ACTION" SWEETENERS

Use "piece of the action" sweeteners to outbid competitors for business. Here's an example:

A professional man died. His practice grossed $100,000 a year. His widow wanted to sell immediately to assure its continuity. A buyer immediately offered her $50,000, payable at $10,000 down, with the balance in equal payments over five years at 5 per cent interest.

A wheeler-dealer, however, outbid this offer. He bought the practice by offering $1,000 cash, $30,000 to be paid over five years at 5 per cent interest, and 10 per cent of the net profit for five years. She will probably end up with more money, but the wheeler-dealer got the valuable practice with a minimal cash outlay.

This demonstrates "piece of the action" tactics for a limited term. When you're buying, limit the terms for piece of the action payout. When you're selling, try to get a continuing piece of the action!

WHEELER-DEALERS ARE PROMOTERS

Wheeler-dealers are promoters. Promoters are, first of all, men of vision who can foresee business possibilities in an idea, a business, a real property, an invention, or any other tangible or intangible entity or a combination of entities.

Second — and this is really what distinguishes a promoter

from a dreamer or a blowhard — a promoter organizes and obtains financing for the new venture or causes the combination (merger) of existing forces for potential profit to take place. The key is seeing the possibility and then organizing it into a reality. The promoter is usually paid for his services with stock, a key job in the new venture, or with cash. A wheeler-dealer may promote to his own account by committing his own resources and taking all the risks (and consequently profits) himself.

A new business can't be started unless there's a promoter. If you start your own business, you're your own promoter. If you start it with other investors, you can get equity, a job or cash compensation without cash outlay. Promotors are breeders of new and bigger businesses.

HOW TO DISCOVER POTENTIAL BIG DEALS

There are several ways to discover potential big deals. Here are just a few:

1. Search for business acquisition opportunities through classifieds, news, business brokers, and business associates. We've discussed classified business opportunities in detail in Chapter Three. The news leads to discovery because it highlights retirements, deaths, and business difficulties that might stimulate the sale of a business. The business broker has an inventory of business for sale. Business associates may know of opportunities that don't make the news.

2. Search for new products and product ideas by studying new products, mechanics, and technical publications. Contact the U.S. Patent Office for information on new patents and "dedicated" patents. Dedicated patents are obtained by companies, foundations, and institutions to advance science and benefit mankind, and to prevent others from obtaining patents on the discovery for exclusive exploitation. Dedicated patents can be used without royalty payment. (Larger libraries may have the Gazette, which lists and describes patents in detail.)

3. Search for "needs" that aren't being met by existing products, and then try to discover or develop a product to fill the need.

4. Search for businesses that can be merged for more profitable operation. Similarity in markets and marketing techniques, in products, or the possibility of reducing overhead may create valid reasons for consolidation.

5. Look for the potential value in big merchandise closeouts and bankruptcy sales. You can sometimes stock a whole store or equip an entire factory for five to fifteen cents on the dollar.

6. Look for real estate opportunities in the classifieds. Explore for run-down business buildings, apartments, and residences. A run-down building in a good area has good upgrading potential.

7. Be alert to special situations that create opportunities. The surplus equipment profits following wars and the science craze after Sputnik are typical examples. New highways, new building developments, changes in mores, economic developments, technical developments and other changes usually create new opportunities.

HOW TO PACKAGE AND PROMOTE BIG DEALS

Your discovery or new idea isn't worth anything till you organize and sell the effort. To promote, you must be able to make things happen. Here's how to package and promote a big deal:

1. Examine your idea. Ask yourself the *what, why, when, where, how, who* questions. These will help you to know it better.

2. Develop a strategy plan for packaging and financing the deal. This plan should answer questions cited in (1) above.

3. Survey the market to confirm your hunches on the proposed venture.

4. Develop a list of possible investors and/or credit sources.

5. With your lawyer, develop a preliminary "Agreement To Organize A Corporation" if the venture is to be incorporated. Determine the number of shares to be authorized, the number to be issued to the initial investors, the par value (if any), your promoter's fee, and estimated time to start.

6. Develop a sales presentation. Support it with charts. Use statistics, graphs, photographs, photos, drawings, analogies, and other illustrative matter that will hold interest and sell. Remember, potential investors are interested in sales and profits. Try to keep it short.

7. Practice your presentation. Use tape recorder and mirror to discover the way to get maximum effect.

8. Set up appointments for presentations or for meetings preliminary to presentations.

9. When your initial stock has been subscribed, get a "Certificate of Incorporation," set up minute books, develop tentative bylaws, and take other necessary steps with the help of your lawyer.

10. Hold a meeting of the corporation and elect your board and chairman. Call for payment of stock subscriptions and authorize issuance of stock. Adopt bylaws and tend to other pertinent matters. Keep minutes of the meeting.

11. Get operations going (See Chapter Seven).

KEEP YOURSELF MOTIVATED WITH GOALS

Keep yourself motivated by choosing major, difficult goals and subdividing them into smaller, easily attainable goals. Many ambitious men end up as nervous wreck failures because they don't know this secret.

The sky's the limit! You can attain any goal you set. Most men actually set them too low, but they're too impatient to reach them and too easily discouraged. Avoid this trap by dividing major goals into many small ones. They're easier to attain. Each time you attain one of your small goals you'll find new courage, enthusiasm, and vitality. Before you know it, you'll have attained major goals. The wheeler-dealer aims high, but he gets there more surely by doing the job in steps!

INCENTIVE PROGRAMS START AT HOME

Reward yourself for your accomplishments. You use incentive programs to motivate employees; now use them to motivate yourself.

Get a new suit when you make the first $1,000.

Get a new car when you make the first $10,000.

Take the world tour with your wife and family when you make the first $50,000.

And give yourself a few perks in-between, too.

Good luck! Actually, you won't need too much if you've mastered the contents of this book and put it to work!